Reclaim Early Childhood: The Philos
Practice of Steiner-Waldorf Early Years Educ

From two very experienced researchers, pedagog ... ...u wi iters we have an interesting, authoritative and insightful book into Steiner Waldorf early childhood education. This book is both practical and educational, filled with useful research, comparative educational practices and a demystifying approach to Steiner's philosophy underpinning the education. I would recommend this book for teachers, parents, educationalists and researchers.

Janni Nicol
Early Childhood Executive Officer, Steiner Waldorf Schools Fellowship (SWSF)

Sebastian and Tamara Suggate suggest that we have abandoned theorizing – by which they mean no-one in the field of Early Childhood Education and Care (ECEC) proposes any large-scale or grand theories any more, as the giants of the last two centuries did – think of Owen, Dewey, Piaget, Bruner, Vygotsky. In *Reclaim Early Childhood* these researchers have provided us with a comprehensive, scholarly and important work based on the ideas of Rudolf Steiner, supported by up-to-date published evidence from many relevant disciplines. The depictions of the nursery settings and the routines of being with and observing children absorbed in exploring life together reminded me of very happy, gentle times early in my career. During the last fifty years, Steiner's writings have been regarded to some extent as questionable, owing to his inclusion of religious elements. One could almost argue that as a result, the mainstream threw the 'baby out with the bathwater' and, again, the Suggates provide thoughtful discussion of Steiner's meanings and intentions here.

The more I read their book, the more I felt heartened because Sebastian and Tamara Suggate have brought us powerful, humane explanations for underpinning our work in the field of ECEC and hopeful arguments against the madness that sadly intrudes on the lives of the young children with whom we work.

Emeritus Professor Tricia David
Canterbury Christchurch University

A wonderful, thoughtful and contemporary book in which the authors bring elegant and apposite research to their subject. The text is illuminating, poetic and practical but never prosaic in its presentation of a compelling case for the relevance of Steiner Waldorf education to children today.

Sally Jenkinson
Co-founder of the Alliance for Childhood, former early years teacher and researcher, lecturer and author of *The Genius of Play*.

The Steiner early years literature has historically been long on beauty, case study and rich phenomenological description, but arguably short in terms of theoretical exposition. This book is a landmark study, not only in the Steiner Waldorf literature but also for early childhood pedagogy more generally. Its authors clearly have a masterful grasp of early childhood and what is and isn't helpful in early child development; and the Steiner-inspired theoretical understanding they bring to this wisdom is unparalleled in the literature. There is no early years practitioner who would not benefit profoundly from reading this path-breaking work – and who wouldn't be inspired to think twice and more about their current practice.

Dr Richard House
Chartered Psychologist, editor of *Too Much, Too Soon? Early Learning and the Erosion of Childhood* and *Childhood, Wellbeing and a Therapeutic Ethos*

This book addresses many of the issues which I and others have worked on for decades, and it is most welcome both for its contemporary look at Waldorf early education and its emphasis on what is needed for a healthy, well-balanced childhood. It fills an important niche in academic circles and among parents who want to deepen their understanding of Waldorf early education and its relevance today.

Joan Almon
Co-founder, Alliance for Childhood and the Waldorf Early Childhood Association of North America

I highly recommend this book for everyone interested in understanding the foundations and scope of Steiner Waldorf early childhood education. Through their experience as researchers, practitioners and parents, Sebastian and Tamara Suggate offer a thoughtful, nuanced description of the essential, health-giving characteristics of Steiner/Waldorf kindergarten education as it comes to expression in diverse cultures around the world. Their description of the challenges for Steiner Education in our times also provides a healthy stimulus for further thought and discussion among teachers, parents, and everyone interested in education as a cultural impulse for our times.

Susan Howard
Coordinator of the Waldorf Early Childhood Association of North America (WECAN), co-founder of the Research Institute for Waldorf Education, and member of the Coordinating Group of the International Association for Steiner Waldorf Early Childhood Education (IASWECE).

To our dear little one,
Who came but did not arrive.

Published by Hawthorn Press, Hawthorn House,
1 Lansdown Lane, Stroud, Gloucestershire, GL5 1BJ, UK
Tel: (01453) 757040   E-mail: info@hawthornpress.com
Website: www.hawthornpress.com

Reclaim Early Childhood © Hawthorn Press 2019
Photographs © Amanda Fisher
Cover design by Lucy Guenot
Typesetting in Adobe Garamond Pro by Winslade Graphics
Printed by Henry Ling Ltd, The Dorset Press, Dorchester

Every effort has been made to trace the ownership of all copyrighted material. If any omission has been made, please bring this to the publisher's attention so that proper acknowledgement may be given in future editions.

The views expressed in this book are not necessarily those of the publisher.

Printed on environmentally friendly chlorine-free paper sourced from renewable forest stock.

British Library Cataloguing in Publication Data applied for

ISBN 978-1-912480-10-4

Reclaim
Early Childhood

The Philosophy, Psychology and Practice of
Steiner-Waldorf Early Years Education

Sebastian Suggate
and
Tamara Suggate

ACKNOWLEDGEMENTS

We would like to thank Martin Large for his enthusiasm in undertaking this book project and Richard House for his careful editing – and both for their encouragement, wise council and patience. Thank you also to Amanda Fisher for capturing the essence of the Waldorf-Steiner environment with her photography. Additionally, we would like to thank the participating kindergartens, educators, parents and families, with a special mention to Rebecca Mitchell, Therese Plöttner, Denise Stevens, the Sunlands Kindergarten (Stroud), the Hereford Steiner Academy and the Cambridge Steiner School. For their insights into kindergarten life around the world, we would like to thank Chandra Kumari Tamang, Joy Levin and Noa Yemini. We are also indebted to Janni Nicol, Jill Taplin and Sally Jenkinson for their thought-provoking conversations and ideas. Cornelia Jachmann was also instrumental in helping conceptualize an earlier publication, from which valuable aspects of her work have flowed into the current work. Finally, this book could not have been written without the help and support of the Weinberger family, our families, and our four daughters who are constantly 'educating' us about the realities of childhood.

Contents

Foreword for the United Kingdom

This book is just what is needed. I recommend it wholeheartedly to those wishing to learn about and answer the important question, 'What is Steiner education all about?'.

The Waldorf-Steiner approach to early childhood education is widely embedded internationally. The book gives reflective illustrations through the descriptions and analysis of practical work in schools located in different parts of the world. This demonstrates the importance placed on developing a culture of openness and reflection. The authors emphasize that the Steiner approach is pedagogical and not evangelical.

The book addresses and critiques issues relating to the dangers of Steinerians adhering to a dogmatic way of working. This is undertaken in a thoroughly modern and rigorous way. So that readers who are not familiar with the Waldorf-Steiner approach are equipped to engage with the arguments offered by the authors, the first part of the book takes them on a journey through the philosophical aspects that are relevant. This, very helpfully, includes the contribution of Plato, Goethe and Kant to the thinking of Steiner. It uses this to unpick what Steiner meant by Anthroposophy. The authors then tease out the meaning of the phenomenological-integrative approach which is central to Steiner's work, and there is a fascinating discussion of the terms Quanta and Qualia in relation to this. A useful distinction is made between quantitative and qualitative approaches which sheds light on Steiner's thinking.

The journey continues with the clarification of 'threefoldness' and a 'whole approach' to education. Young children are seen to seek out and experience the world in its entirety. Words which can be difficult and might be viewed as old fashioned and narrow in this day and age are explained, such as 'spirit', 'soul', 'body' and 'will'. Steiner sees these as different sides of the same phenomenon, and not to be viewed in isolation. Throughout the book the traditional terminology is lifted out of any possibility of ossification and scrutinized in the context of current science, psychology and other disciplines.

The authors emphasize that the focus of Steiner's approach was to bring about 'sharpening of the mind'. It certainly does that, linking the reader with Steiner's connection not just to education, but also to medicine and agriculture in ways which have current relevance. There is a strong and steady message that education should remove fixed judgements or a static and stuck view of the child or adult learner. Instead, Steiner education is about a state of 'becoming'.

There is also discussion of the fact that the phenomenological-empirical and integrative view of the child held by Steiner has not made its way into mainstream education in an embedded way.

A large part of the book then takes the reader into the regular practices of the Steiner approach. Freehood is considered and linked to current thinking about executive functioning and autonomy. There is considerable space devoted to the Steiner approach to play and imagination. The importance of imitation and the adult as a powerful role model is introduced, and rhythm, structure and safety are given attention. Language that involves over-explanation or which restricts children by outer compulsion is critiqued. When it is 'dry, abstract, relentless', it is seen to work in 'a parching way'.

The Steiner approach is, throughout the book, discussed by the authors in ways which connect it to current research in education. This is used both to support Steiner and to critique other approaches. But there is respect for the pioneering work of educators such as Froebel and Montessori, and Steiner is located in relation to them, just as in the earlier part of the book there is consideration of other philosophical approaches to educating young children. The points raised are not judgemental or pursued with a silo mentality.

The authors do not avoid taking a serious look at some of the recent criticisms of Steiner's work. They push back at most of these and give evidence for doing so. They also see where there is a need to be pragmatic in ways which keep the authenticity of Steiner's voice without departing from his principles. For this reason there is a full section investigating the digital aspects, and the approach to early literacy.

This is a brave book, not afraid to examine with integrity and a scholarly determination and practical expertise the work of one of the most respected pioneer educators in the Western world, whose approach has also spread to other parts of the world. The authors make the point that 'To understand children one has to understand oneself and the effects we have on children in our care'. They demonstrate in this book how the Steiner approach to the education of children in the first seven years needs to be about developing a culture of openness and reflection, so that it can find a place in any ethnic community or culture if there are willing parents and educators.

I could not put this book down.

Professor Tina Bruce, CBE
Honorary Professor of Early Childhood Education, University of Roehampton, 2019

Foreword for North America

This year, 2019, marks the 100th anniversary of the founding of Waldorf education based on the insights of Rudolf Steiner (1861–1925). The first school was created at the request of the workers of the Waldorf Astoria cigarette factory in Stuttgart, Germany. Since then, Waldorf schools have seen a steady rise, with some notable set-backs. During the Nazi era, all Waldorf schools were closed in countries occupied by the National Socialists, but they reopened quickly when World War II came to an end. When Communism came to an end there was an explosion of interest in Russia and the former Soviet countries where Waldorf had been forbidden for decades. When apartheid came to an end in South Africa, there was a surge of interest in Waldorf early childhood education in the townships. Now there is huge interest in China, where hundreds of teachers are enrolled in Waldorf teacher training programs.

During its 100-year history, Waldorf has changed and adapted to each new stage of its life. Yet its devotion to a well-balanced education based on a deep understanding of a child's development has remained constant. This book addresses both elements: the underlying understanding of the child, as well as the diverse ways to apply such an understanding in different cultures.

Today, there are over 1,000 Waldorf or Steiner Schools, and nearly 2,000 Waldorf early childhood programs in more than 70 countries. They are independent of each other yet work closely together in national and international associations.

Over the years many books have been written about Waldorf education. In the early childhood field most focus on practical aspects of the education. This book is different. It includes descriptions of the practice of Waldorf early education, but it primarily focuses on the underlying ideas of the education and the ways its approach links to educational and scientific theories of our time. For instance, the section on the senses connects Rudolf Steiner's view that there are 12 senses with current neurological thinking about the many senses of the human being, all of which need to be cultivated in a well-balanced child.

Also, this book goes beyond focusing on Waldorf education. As the authors state in their introductory chapter, 'This book is as much a defence of childhood as it is an advocacy of Steiner education'. This defence of childhood comes at an extremely important time. In my 50 years of working with and for children, I have never seen a time of greater need to defend childhood, especially in the United States where I have been active. There is a growing materialistic view of the world and this applies to children, as well. Rather than paying attention to the way children actually develop and then creating educational approaches that support the child's healthy development, the child is viewed in a machine-like way, and arbitrary goals for achievement are set as if one can simply recalibrate the child to perform tasks at ages we arbitrarily decree.

In the United States, we see this tendency especially in the new Common Core standards that require children to read basic books with 'purpose and understanding' by the end of kindergarten. Some children are capable of this task, but many are not developmentally ready, and suffer from this unreasonable demand. Those setting the standards claim they are evidence-based, but in fact there is no evidence that says that teaching reading in kindergarten leads to better reading and comprehension skills by third or fourth grade. Early gains, which do take place, are quickly lost, but the effect of the pressure which the children experience in preschool and kindergarten is not so easily lost. It can create anxiety and tension, which can then interfere with developing a love of reading and of learning in general.

Efforts to speed up young children's development can result in serious stress. We currently see increases in physical and mental health problems among children, which many associate with the growing stress of childhood today. The decline in children's health and well-being concerned me so deeply that after 30 years as a Waldorf early childhood educator, I enlarged my focus and co-founded the Alliance for Childhood, a broad-based organization comprised of educators, health professionals, play advocates, and many others who are deeply concerned about the plight of children today. The Alliance has focused on issues such as the over-use of electronic media in childhood, the ill-effects of too much academic instruction in preschool and kindergarten, and the need to restore creative play in children's lives.

This book addresses many of the issues which I and others have worked on for decades, and it is most welcome both for its contemporary look at Waldorf early education and its emphasis on what is needed for a healthy, well-balanced childhood. It fills an important niche in academic circles and among parents who want to deepen their understanding of Waldorf early education and its relevance today.

Joan Almon
College Park, Maryland, USA
February 2019

Prologue

On the first Sunday of December – although winter this year had not yet really taken hold – a light covering of snow lies on the ground. As the afternoon wears on, growing greyer by the minute, the pristine, almost luminescent blanket of snow appears to glisten in contrast to the gathering dusk. Coats and woolly hats, scarves and snowsuits drawn tight at the neck attempt to hold the cold at bay. Although only weakly illuminated by dim candlelight, the kindergarten building, with its angular yet organic forms gradually dissolving into the oncoming dusk, invitingly draws guests into its midst. Upstairs in the main room, parents have exchanged their coats for the quiet murmur of anticipation.

In the middle of the room a large spiral formed from pine tree cuttings is laid out with a single upright candle placed in the centre. To the right of the window a harpist is seated, beneath the barely visible silhouette of an oak tree – the very one that shaded the children during the hot summer days.

Quietly at first, initially accompanied by just a few of the parents and teachers, the lyrics of 'Little Donkey' weave their way into consciousness, increasing in volume as the children tentatively enter the candlelit room and take their seats. Some faces bear grins, still more beam with pride, others peer and gaze towards the seated parents. A moment of quite follows, before the young harpist begins to fill the room with the delicate tones of Albinoni's Adagio. A peaceful, majestic mood reigns, the melancholy, beauty and hope in centre-stage.

A teacher picks up an apple, the centre of which has been carved out and replaced with a small beeswax candle, and walks slowly with it to the middle of the spiral. There, she lights her own candle from that which burns brightly in the heart of the room, before walking back a small way and carefully placing the apple down amongst the pine sprigs. The room now glows just a little brighter. One after another, each child follows the same path, some children ambling slowly and dreamily, others purposefully and energetically, some smiling coyly at their parents as they go, before placing their candles at various points along the spiral. Each child, with unique gait and personality, purpose and pace, enriches the room with a flame, until the wintery darkness is almost overcome by the warm, gentle flickering light emanating from the spiral.

Universe and child, light and darkness, music and art, movement and stillness. What is Steiner education all about?

CHAPTER 1

Introduction: Education to Meet the Needs of the Child and the Times?

> How education proceeds from this point will transform society, or
> send it plummeting back into the savagery of the dark ages.
> *(Sardello and Sanders, 1999, pp. 244–245)*

Of the many paradoxes of recent times, one stands out perhaps above all others. Childhood is revered and respected – and yet also subjugated and ignored – like never before. Hardly any other area of life is the recipient of such lofty and benevolent praise in the abstract, while falling victim to banality and neglect in practice. Barbaric practices such as child labour and corporal punishment may have been eradicated in much of the (Western) world, yet childhood remains well and truly under threat – for childhood is misunderstood.

When we contrast the state of childhood, of being children, with our adult conceptions and shadowy memories for how it was 'to be young', this discrepancy becomes comprehensible. Our memories are often verbally dominated, and thus it is perhaps no wonder that our conceptions of childhood are also clothed in concepts and terms. The path back to understanding childhood is thus achieved through an overcoming of this abstract scaffolding to begin to see and experience the reality of childhood underneath. For this, we require – alongside the scientific, legalistic and pragmatic – an inherently phenomenological approach to childhood. This is precisely what the founder of Waldorf-Steiner education endeavoured to do.

Indeed, because life itself is so complex, and arguably increasingly so, an appropriate education that can meet the full reality of modern life must also be inherently complex. Perhaps only through an attempt to observe the world exactly, investigating its many riddles with integrity, can the initially hidden threads linking many phenomena together be slowly discovered. Bearing this in mind, it is not surprising that before Waldorf education could be founded by Steiner, he had first to found his approach to knowledge out of which practical answers to the riddles of life could slowly be developed. Perhaps the unique feature of Steiner education, if not its defining characteristic, is that at its heart lie decades of struggle by its founder, Rudolf Steiner, to understand the riddles of human existence. This approach to knowledge he termed 'anthroposophy', and the attempt to understand child development and education out of this leads to Steiner-Waldorf education.

This book is as much a defence of childhood as it is an advocacy of Steiner education. We seek to lay down and make explicit the principles for child development and a corresponding early childhood education that addresses the needs of children, and that deepens what is understood, integrating research across many disciplines, all the while stimulating further thought and initiative. No education approach has the right to rest on its laurels, clothed in a mantel of self-congratulation and dogma, but through its deeds it must prove itself again and again, one child at a time, accepting the new challenges and developments that individually and collectively arise.

The idea for the current publication originally arose from an introductory German text written by the first author in 2015. We soon realised that an expanded and more comprehensive text in English would not be without merit. Our aim in writing this book was to fundamentally take the principles and practice of early years Steiner education and comprehensively illustrate these in a fashion to which the modern reader can relate. Too often we encounter people who say that they are interested in, or even connected to, Steiner education, but that they have difficulty finding literature that is written in an accessible way, incorporating other conceptions and scientific work, while not shying away from the spiritual-philosophical foundations. Our intention is that people from many different walks of life may find a way of relating to the ideas presented here, even those who may initially find the use of the word 'spirit' troublesome. This is perhaps an ambitious undertaking, but one that we hope to have at least partly achieved with our contribution. Our intention takes nothing away from the many existing works on this topic – often more practice-oriented – which this book seeks to complement rather than to replace. Many of these are referenced throughout, and we encourage the reader to extend his or her understanding of specific areas by referring to such previous literature.

Our aim is to demonstrate the relevance of Steiner early childhood education in the modern world. Some people may perceive this form of education as old-fashioned and out-dated – where are the electronic toys, I-Pads and other marvels of the modern world? But it is precisely in the current climate that the progressive elements of Waldorf education, with its truly humane understanding of childhood, anchored in deep philosophy, sustainable education, common sense and practical aesthetics – in short, covering everything from Plato to play silks – are needed.

In writing this book, we deliberately limited the scope to traditional kindergarten age children, namely, ages three to six. As the modern world changes, the demand for childcare starting at significantly earlier ages is obviously also increasing. Some Steiner institutions have responded to this demand by opening groups specifically designed to address the needs of the younger child, but such considerations are beyond the scope of the current book. However, the principles outlined here can be used to guide practice for these younger children also. At this juncture, a note on our adopted nomenclature. At different times we have used the term 'Waldorf-Steiner kindergartens' as well as 'Steiner kindergartens' and 'Waldorf kindergartens'. This seems sensible, not least because it is useful to give readers the full range of nomenclature used in the field. These terms are interchangeable, therefore, and all refer to the same phenomenon.

Education is a life-long process, and we anticipate (and certainly hope!) that many years from now, we may be wiser than today, and certain passages or ideas in this book may no longer be current or consistent with our developing understanding. In this vein, we request that our words not be written in stone, and we reserve the right to change our minds, and encourage you, dear reader, to do so too, using each child as the only true book in which the principles of education are inscribed.

In a Nutshell

- An education is needed that grasps the essence of childhood.

- The time for advocacy and partisanship in education is over; instead, times call for a deep and flexible responsibility to the challenges presented to childhood.

- Steiner-Waldorf has the potential to pave the way, so long as she is open and self-critical, not resting on any (false) laurels.

CHAPTER 2

The Anthroposophical Foundation Demystified

2.1 Education arising from philosophy

> The problem here is not that there [is] anything wrong with saying that it is the job of schools and teachers to pass on knowledge and skills conducive to effective individual and/or social functioning, success or flourishing, but that more needs to be thought and said about what constitutes such success or flourishing if we are to avoid dangerously narrow or attenuated conceptions of education and schooling.
>
> *(Carr, 2012, p. 28)*

Both modern and ancient thinkers have argued that education without philosophy is often a form of – or may soon end up in – tyranny (Carr, 2012). In Plato's dialogues, Socrates addresses this problem in critiquing the Sophists, who teach useful knowledge and skills simply for profit, with little regard to the virtue or moral development of their pupils. A similar approach to the Sophists appears to have been adopted by large tracts of modern educational curricula and governments, with their strong focus on skills relevant for the economy (Labaree, 2014). Exemplifying this, the European Commission recently claimed that discussions on the purpose of education were now finished: the purpose is simply to serve the economy (Dahlin, 2012). This adult-centred way of thinking about education has become seemingly detached from the nature of children, not stopping to, as small children do, repeatedly ask: 'But why…?'

Even if one formulates ideas about what education should achieve beyond serving the economy, the ensuing ideals and aims often become too abstract, or take on the form of slogans that are difficult to implement, or which in and of themselves mean little. Examples of such slogans are perhaps that education should be for: 'all', 'social justice', 'tomorrow's world', or 'the whole human being'. The end-result of such slogans is often formulating ideals, standards and competencies that children should acquire, with education then becoming the process of fitting children into such abstract ideals (Steiner, 1924/2004).

Nor is it particularly fruitful to expound truisms, such as 'let children be children' or 'educate for democracy and tolerance'. Although on the surface such 'progressive' statements sound nice, do they allow us to defend childhood if we cannot say exactly why a child is different from an adult? Does education for democracy mean that citizens need to function in society, simply vote once every few years and pay taxes (i.e. collectivism), rise up against state-sanctioned (kratos) injustice, or conform to the will of the demos (Greek for people)? What is tolerance, and how do we educate children to tolerance without generating indifference?

Currently, if one looks at government educational webpages from around the world, idealistic aims of education (e.g. tolerance, freedom, democracy) are stated alongside utilitarian ones (e.g. learning to read, supporting the economy). The former are nearly impossible to measure and dictate through policy, whereas the latter can be reduced to a narrow range of skills that can be taught and tested. The consequence for education tends to involve propelling this towards focusing on an increasingly narrow array of standards (i.e. reading, writing and science) that have clear practical utility (House, 2007).

Although certainly difficult, reflection on what the purpose of education should be needs to comprise the very first step in any formulation of education (Cahn, 2009). Indeed, Steiner education arose out of Rudolf Steiner's struggles with age-old questions, such as: Are thinking and knowledge objective? Do we possess free will? What is the soul or psyche and human 'I'? How do psychological states relate to physical states? How exactly are children different from adults? – and so on.

As will be outlined in this book, Steiner developed detailed ideas about the human being, on the nature of knowledge, freedom and truth, which form the philosophical groundwork of many of the principles in Steiner education. His philosophy was called anthroposophy: hence, just as education arises ideally from philosophy, anthroposophy arises from his philosophy, which we turn to next.

2.2 Anthroposophy arising from philosophy

> By the turn of the century, a split had occurred, into a soulless neurology and a bodiless psychology.
>
> *(Sacks, 2015, p. 98)*

In the decades before Steiner education arose, the Austrian philosopher Rudolf Steiner spent much time outlining what he believed to be an approach to studying the world that had the potential to extend human understanding both downwards into the details of physical existence, and upwards, or into the more hidden workings and laws of the universe. He sought to combine: (a) a science of ideas as expounded by the likes of Plato and Pythagoras, with (b) a detailed observation of the world, as advocated by Aristotle and empirical science, via (c) an eminently phenomenological, experienced-based approach, in the sense of Goethe and the phenomenologists of the twentieth century.

For his approach to knowledge he adopted the term 'anthroposophy', which is derived from the ancient Greek words 'ánthrōpos' (human) and 'sophía' (wisdom). As mentioned earlier, anthroposophy is intended to provide an approach for better understanding life itself, which renders it, by definition, complex! Furthermore, because much of that which constitutes life is essentially invisible – such as memory, experience, thought, idea, emotion, mental image – anthroposophy necessarily delves into the realms of the invisible. Furthermore, another often overlooked point to note is that Steiner intended his epistemology to complement other approaches to knowledge. In no way was it intended that anthroposophical insights render those of other fields – be it psychology, biology, or even artificial intelligence – redundant (Steiner, 1917/1996).

One might well justifiably ask at this point, why do we need something like anthroposophy when millions of researchers and practitioners are working across the world to constantly provide new insight and improve human existence on this planet? Modern science has enabled countless important discoveries of primarily the physical world. Nearly every square inch of the Earth's surface has been mapped, and matter and anatomy are being examined in ever-smaller detail. Brain and organic processes are being investigated with increasing sophistication.

Although there is undoubtedly still more of the physical world to discover, it has been argued that the next horizons to be explored are psychological-intellectual or soul-spiritual in nature (Lievegoed, 1985). Evidence of this need arises from the still primitive treatments available for the epidemic of psychological disturbances (House and Loewenthal, 2008). Similarly, our understanding of matters of the mind is still very much in its infancy. To illustrate this point, we still do not understand where logic comes from and how it comes to be such a reliable, eternal and steadfast companion, fundamental for knowledge and society. Similarly, there is still no accepted definition of what a number is (Rosenberg, 2012). Studies of the human brain recognize a complexity that matches that of the entire universe. As these simple examples show, the next important voyages of discovery will likely involve deepening our understanding of ourselves, which is precisely a goal of anthroposophy (Lievegoed, 1985).

A second reason for developing additional approaches to knowledge is that scientific progress can be extremely slow regarding the animate world, especially in the field of education. Educational research, when conducted empirically, tends to lead to a focus on quick and measurable gains (Suggate, 2015) – at the expense of a more patient, long-term approach as found, for example, in Steiner education. As discussed later, there are compelling empirical findings pointing to the harm that can be caused by focusing on short-term, measurable academic gains instead of guiding children in their development, like a gardener patiently does, intervening only as necessary. However, these empirical findings require decades of research, by which time 'progress' has flooded early education with new and 'better' programmes whose true effects also require decades of research to understand. An example here is the focus on digital learning – with technological giants able to develop products far more quickly than science is able to investigate their long-term effects. Clearly, we cannot always wait until empirical science has conducted decades of work and debate before embarking on educational reform. Instead, we need an approach to observing the child that is schooled in empirical reality but which arises out of a more sensitive observational ability. This also is a goal of anthroposophy.

In his last year of life, Steiner defined anthroposophy as 'a path of knowledge and development that sought to lead the spiritual in the individual human to the spiritual in the world' (Steiner, 1925/1989, p. 14). To do so, we must cultivate hard knowledge of both ourselves and the world around us, that recognizes both the physical and the psychological-intellectual realms of existence. Some readers may query the use of the term 'spirituality' when we have just argued that anthroposophy seeks to represent a scientific path to knowledge. However, before addressing the place of the spirit in science and education, let us first expand on what is meant here by the term 'spirit'.

The English word 'spirit' originates from the Latin word 'spiritus', which is connected with breath, air, soul and life. In Steiner's mother tongue, the German word for 'spirit' is Geist, which has a broader meaning than in English, encompassing both 'spirit' and 'intellect'. Because Geist in German relates to both thinking and a less tangible essence (more similar to the English meaning of spiritus), it is easier in the German language to show how these two principles are potentially related, as the German idealistic philosophers tried to do. In English, however, the word 'spirit' has come to have abstract, religious connotations, and often evokes a negative reaction in people who perceive the term as being connected with a lack of rational, scientific thought. As discussed in more detail in later sections (see Chapter 3), the spirit as here intended can be understood as that part of the human being that is able to experience, often through thinking, that part of existence that relates to eternal, invisible but nonetheless 'solid' ideas. One particularly clear example of such ideas is those found in mathematics; although, for example, a negative number is nowhere to be 'seen', it is still a generally accepted concept with proven use (at least for mathematicians and engineers).

A similar approach to anthroposophy can be found in the emerging discipline of phenomenology. Although phenomenology has many different forms developed by diverse thinkers, including Goethe, Sartre, Husserl and Heidegger, there are some common features that are also important for anthroposophy. First, the mind, or conscious experience, is seen as the starting point of inquiry, not an abstract law or hypothesis that is first projected into reality. Secondly, phenomenology tries to direct the mind to experiencing the various things of the world in their entirety before beginning to dissect these and theorize about them. Thirdly, any given phenomenon is seen as being experienced in a number of different ways and on a number of (potentially infinite!) different levels – a number is both a certain collection of objects and a mathematical building block or law, for example. A human being has a body, but also has psychological and intellectual-spiritual states too. Thus, to phenomenology, one side alone – usually the physical and quantitative one – should not dominate scientific considerations, but should always be considered along with other dimensions. Fourthly, at least in the phenomenology developed by Goethe and Steiner, our limits to knowledge are created by our limits to consciousness – something which has evolved historically, however, and will continue to do so.

As one first step, this phenomenology calls us to then go beyond theories and approach 'the source of thoughts' (Petitmengin, 2007) themselves, which may bring us to look more closely at the nature of thinking itself (Dahlin, 2009). Perhaps such an approach will allow us to develop educational ideas that arise directly out of the needs of children as these phenomenologically represent the needs of the times.

2.3 Education arising from anthroposophy

It is not our goal to teach ideology in the Waldorf school, though such a thought might easily occur to people when hearing that anthroposophists have established a new school. Our goal is to carry our understanding gained through [anthroposophy] right into practical teaching.
(Steiner, 1921–1922/2003, p. 125)

For many people, the first question that arises upon hearing of Steiner education is how can it be scientific and appropriate to our times when it is based on an anthroposophical foundation with its spiritual character – which makes it 'religious' and hence 'unscientific'. As discussed throughout this book, a very good many practices in Steiner education are supported by empirical evidence, even when the Zeitgeist has been pushing hard in the other direction. Examples include: (a) the benefits of free play; (b) the positive effects of story-telling; (c) the value of incorporating nature, aesthetics and art into education; (d) the importance of physical movement for learning and development; (e) the dangers of electronic media; (f) fostering imagination; (g) the full recognition of imitation in early childhood; (h) the links between educational experiences and health; and (i) the importance of human relationships in learning. Indeed, these aspects have been at various times – or still are! – entirely absent from mainstream education.

Throughout this book, we refer to the idea that the anthroposophical approach to knowledge can be understood as a kind of self-education and self-development. According to this notion, the human being needs to develop new faculties to investigate new phenomena. The faculties that need developing depend on whether the phenomenon in question is a sense-perceptible or an intellectual or even spiritual one. In the physical sciences, equipment is used to extend human perception into domains that were previously not able to be perceived (e.g. the electron microscope, and the infrared camera). In the 'spiritual' sciences or humanities, such as philosophy or mathematics, the development of faculties of logic and the ability to think in and perceive mathematical laws can be learned.

In his book *Riddles of the Soul* (Steiner, 1917/1996), Steiner specified what he believed to be the relationship between anthroposophy and sciences that have physical sensory impressions as their starting point. These physical sciences provide sensory input that forms the content of mental images. In modern psychological and philosophical language, these mental images would be called 'constructs' or 'representations'. These mental images are subjective representations of reality, based on an objective world existing outside, which is perceived by the senses. However, there is also a subtle, internal world that has its own rules, forming the representations from the 'inside'.

If we closely observe this inner subjective world of mental representations, it is possible to notice that there is also an influence from an inner objective source alongside the outer one that we know as the physical world. This inner world is most noticeable for the modern human, in its manifestation in the laws of logic. In the world of mental images, even this objective inner world of logic reigns supreme. To illustrate the supremacy of objective inner worlds, try imagining a logical impossibility, such as a triangle with five corners, a colour that is bright pink and bright blue at the same time, or a single number that is both positive and negative.

Steiner saw no reason why science should confine itself to physical facts simply because only 'physical' instruments were recognized as objective. Instead, he maintained that we have to simply find the right instruments for psychological-intellectual phenomena as well. The great philosopher Immanuel Kant (1724–1804), whose ideas are still very influential today, was of the opinion that there were clear limits to our knowledge. Everything that could not be investigated with physical instruments and logic was an issue of faith. From an educational point of view, this means that certain questions remain difficult to investigate once these transgress Kant's boundaries of knowledge. For Steiner, following from Goethe, the question was rather, how we can develop the faculties that we need to investigate previously inaccessible questions. Steiner believed, accordingly, that there should be no boundaries to knowledge (Steiner, 1918/1986): everything was a question of development. And herein lies the need for anthroposophy alongside psychology, sociology and anthropology.

To summarize, a sound education that does not fall into abstract idealism or unreflected pragmatism needs to be built on careful contemplation and inquiry on both the purpose of education and the nature of the human being itself. In contrast with our impressive conquering of the external physical world, we are but dabbling fools in exploring our psychological-intellectual lives. Here we depend on logic, mathematics, memory, intuition – without being able to say what these really are, or how they arise. To do so requires new advances in self-knowledge, which is what Steiner tried to initiate with his anthroposophy. Based on his insight, he detailed his understanding of the human being, which we will discuss after presenting a brief sketch of Steiner's life. In short, the anthroposophical approach has two key implications for education. First, Steiner education is based on a thorough phenomenological-anthroposophical observation of human experience. Secondly, this method of observation leads to the recognition of both spiritual and psychological aspects of human existence alongside physical ones. Both have to be cultivated with the exactitude and creativity with which modern empirical science sets about its tasks.

2.4 A short sketch of Rudolf Steiner's life and work

Although Rudolf Steiner died before the first Waldorf kindergartens became established, his work forms, without question, the foundation of this educational approach. Steiner was born on the 25 February 1861 in Kraljevic, a village formerly part of the Austro-Hungarian empire but now situated in modern day Serbia. His family relocated frequently during his childhood, as his father worked for the Austrian train service. Despite having to travel daily for up to three hours on foot to school, Steiner read widely, teaching himself languages, which allowed him to tutor other students in order to supplement the meagre family income. Philosophy played a prominent role in his reading list, especially Immanuel Kant and, later, Johann Wolfgang von Goethe, and he was also particularly fascinated by geometry and mathematics.

After finishing school, he attended the University of Applied Sciences in Vienna (1879–1882), where he began his career writing philosophical and cultural works. From 1884 to 1890 Steiner worked as a tutor for the Specht family, where he was responsible for educating their intellectually disabled ten year-old son Otto, who suffered from hydrocephalus. When Steiner began working with Otto, he hardly seemed capable of learning, having only acquired 'reading, writing, and arithmetic in a most rudimentary form' (Steiner, 1925, p. 84). In his time with Steiner, Otto not only soon caught up in his subjects but he also excelled to such a degree that he later went on to study medicine and qualify as a doctor. Steiner wrote that his time tutoring Otto provided 'a rich source of learning' with some of the acquired knowledge later metamorphosing into the guiding principles of Steiner education. Steiner wrote of this time:

> I had to find access to a soul which was in a kind of sleeping state that gradually had to be enabled to gain mastery over its bodily manifestations. In a certain sense, one had first to awaken the soul within the body. I was thoroughly convinced that the boy really had great, although hidden, mental capacities.... This educational task became to me the source from which I myself learned very much. Through the method of instruction which I had to apply, there was laid open to my view the association between the spiritual-mental and the bodily in man. There I went through my real course of study in physiology and psychology.
>
> *(ibid., S. 84–5, translation adapted*
> *by the authors from wn.rsarchive.org)*

Based on a recommendation from Steiner's friend and mentor, the professor Karl Julius Schröer (1825–1900), he was nominated to edit Goethe's natural scientific writing. As with his time in Vienna, this new activity in Weimar – a cultural and geographical centre of Germany in the late nineteenth century – bought Steiner into contact with many prominent personalities in the blossoming literature and art movements of the time. In 1892, Steiner received a doctorate in philosophy for his work, the essence of which was later published in one of his most widely read books *The philosophy of freedom*.[1] In this work, Steiner attempted to lay the philosophical foundations for using our thinking to rise to a spiritual world view resting on solid scientific foundations, from which humankind could learn to become truly free.

Between finishing his doctorate in 1892 and the founding of the first Waldorf-Steiner school in Stuttgart in 1919, Steiner lived first in Berlin and then in Dornach in Switzerland. This intervening period saw him lecture in a workers' school, edit a literary and culture journal, head the German section of the Theosophical Society before being displaced because of his failure to comply with its ever-growing anti-Western streak, produce many written philosophical works, hold thousands of lectures around Europe, and found the Anthroposophical Society. Prior to his death on 30 March 1925, Steiner wrote and lectured on multifaceted topics relating to the fields of medicine, agriculture, education and special education, philosophy, architecture, eurythmy, theology, Christology, natural science, history and psychology. This work is reflected today in a very large number of institutions, including: biodynamic farms, Steiner schools, special schools, anthroposophical medical practices, the Christian Community and higher education institutions.

The first Waldorf-Steiner school was founded in Stuttgart during the catastrophic year directly after the end of the First World War. Emil Molt was the owner of a large cigarette factory and was concerned about the well-being of not only his workers, but about society as a whole. After attempts to improve the working conditions and cultural life of his workers, he came to the conclusion that a new educational approach was needed before sustainable societal change was possible. Molt then asked Steiner about the possibility of founding a new school, which soon gave rise to the Waldorf education movement, named after Molt's Waldorf-Astoria cigarette factory.

Subsequently, Steiner began to lecture more systematically on his ideas about education, not only in Germany but also particularly in Holland and England. There are many fascinating accounts of his visits to the first Waldorf school. He would involve himself in many different capacities – from jumping in to take over lessons, observing children and instruction, meeting with individual students, advising and supporting the teachers, and helping with the development of the school. By all accounts he was greatly admired by the students and teachers, and he could often be seen walking down the corridor smiling to himself after being in the classroom. It is believed that the school and corresponding educational approach was the favourite of all the initiatives arising out of his philosophy (Lindenberg, 1997).

On New Year's Eve of 1922/1923, the nearly completed first Goetheanum was burned to the ground in an arson attack, which constituted a very significant blow for Steiner. The Goetheanum was a building that Steiner and others had built on a donated piece of land in Dornach (near Basel, Switzerland). The building had a wooden construction, much of it carved by Steiner and his colleague's own hands, embodying a new form of 'organic' architecture. Many reports indicate that this event affected Steiner greatly, with his health suffering immensely (ibid.). Nevertheless, after expending every available effort to put the fire out until the smouldering ashes were greeted by the first sunrise of the New Year, a determined Steiner insisted that work must continue, and his programme of lectures continued on that very day. Recognizing several deficiencies in the Anthroposophical Society, Steiner re-founded this society one year after the Goetheanum fire, and was elected as its head. In the next nine months his activity was still more intense, travelling frequently and maintaining a busy schedule of lecturing and writing on a diverse range of topics, visiting and advising the growing initiatives in medicine, agriculture, education and religious renewal, and making plans for the building of a new Goetheanum. In September of 1924, however, his activity was abruptly halted due to deteriorating health, and he died on 30 March of the following year.

Steiner was, and remains, a controversial figure, evoking a broad spectrum of reactions. Some people look on his life's work with astonishment, struck by the number of new initiatives he developed, his depth of knowledge and insight into many diverse fields, and his human qualities of humour, self-sacrifice and attempts at cultivating a cultural impulse to raise post-war Europe out of its misery. Others see in him a significant person and respect the fruits of his work but themselves have difficulty relating to the perceived 'mysticism' or the strong spirituality in his work. A small number of vocal critiques – and a cursory search of the internet bears testament to this – simply reject his ideas out of hand, and scour his work searching for statements that can be used to argue that Steiner education and anthroposophy are dangerous. Finally, there are a small number of scholars who work academically with Steiner's work, and a growing number of empirical publications testing aspects of Steiner's approaches in medicine, education and agriculture.

In a Nutshell

- The purpose and philosophy of education need to inform how we educate.

- One approach to understanding the purpose is to understand humanity. This leads from philosophy, to anthroposophy, to education.

- Rudolf Steiner founded anthroposophy to focus and develop our abilities to attend to subtle yet crucial aspects of humanity that are often ignored.

- Such crucial aspects include acknowledging and exploring our mental life, which can provide a new source for insight into the riddles of education.

CHAPTER 3

The Anthroposophical View
of the Human Being

The question of what a human being actually is, is not only complicated, but has wide-reaching implications for education. Usually, two positions are quickly discernible. Atheists maintain that the human being comprises a material, physical body that is solely responsible for human existence. In contrast, theists argue that alongside the body, the human being also possesses an immortal soul. Briefly considered, both positions are philosophically problematic. The theist position often suffers a lack of detail in explaining what a soul is actually like and how it can influence our actions if it is entirely different in substance to our body (e.g. a ghost driving a car?). This problem is known as dualism, and has been much debated since the philosopher Descartes proposed his Cartesian dualism, whereby soul and body are comprised of two different substances, a thinking and a material substance (Descartes, 1647/2012).

On the other hand, the atheist position has difficulty in explaining how something physical – that is the mere 2½ pounds of brain that we have – can create something that is non-physical, namely experience (of quality, thoughts, emotions etc.). Indeed, despite decades of memory research, we seem even further away from understanding how or where an essential and nearly unlimited human capacity for memory is stored (Gallistel and Balsam, 2014; Trettenbrein, 2016). Similarly, we at best only understand which parts of the brain are active when we think, but not what *causes* the thoughts.

Steiner, among others, went beyond both of these positions, and argued that the human being needs to be studied in detail with the appropriate methods in order to determine how our inner life relates to our body and the surrounding world (Steiner, 1918/1986). Through doing so, Steiner maintained that the human being was not one-fold as argued by atheists, nor two-fold as advocated by Cartesian theists, but three-fold, comprising a spirit in addition to having a body and a soul. What is his justification for speaking of not only a soul but a spirit as well?

Before considering the plausibility of this threefold conception of the human being, two discussions are necessary. First, we need to outline a way of investigating and thinking about the human being that leads to this three-fold conception. For this approach we draw on the discipline of phenomenology. Secondly, it is important to be clear about what is meant by the terms body, soul and spirit. Over two thousand years of heated philosophical, religious and scientific debate – at times boiling over into unthinkable slaughter committed by both theists and atheists – have left these terms emotionally laden. This history still lives on in our language and conceptions! Therefore, we ask the reader to first attempt to lay aside preconceptions as we try to formulate what we intend with the words 'body', 'soul', and 'spirit'. Although the following section may seem unduly complicated and initially unrelated to education, the considerations do, we believe, provide the building blocks upon which to build a solid education.

3.1 A phenomenological excursion

Nothing is inside, nothing is outside,
For that which is inside is also outside,
Thus grasp without delay,
The divine revealed openly.

— *Johann Wolfgang von Goethe*

Needless to say, we also do not have the answer to the age-old riddle of what a human being is. Nor, necessarily, did Steiner; but his detailed descriptions are nonetheless worth close consideration. One particular hurdle to viewing the nature of the human being with ever-increasing objectivity is that we often forget the starting point in our thinking – or put another way, *what* is doing the thinking.

In fact, perhaps the most pervasive and erroneous form of this occurs in considering what we term 'reality'. Most Western-educated people consider reality to be that which can be experienced through the senses, as opposed to that which exists as consciousness. When traced back historically, this was not always the case. Philosophically, the shift in Western thought was initiated by the empiricists (e.g. Hume and Locke) in departure from Plato and Descartes, who placed more trust in ideas (e.g. mathematics).

Returning to the modern Western-educated person's understanding of reality, we could express this more precisely and say that it is not simply that we trust our senses to convey reality, but that we find sense information imbued with some kind of objective verification to be particularly compelling. For example, we believe it is warm if the thermometer reads 30 degrees Celsius, our last night's sleep was poor if we were woken three times by a child, or if the economy grows at 2.4 per cent instead of 1.4 per cent then we feel the country is more prosperous. That is, we are socialized to mix quantities (e.g. temperature measurements) with qualities (e.g. the perception of warmth) in many domains of life such that slowly, we cannot distinguish between them, unless we stop to examine our presuppositions. Indeed, a major feature of current education and modern society is that we learn to measure experiences, to objectify and quantify *qualities* from an ever-earlier age. This, in and of itself, is not necessarily problematic, and constitutes a vastly important cultural development, although it can lead to the most fundamental errors in thinking. How so?

Applied to understanding the human being, this fundamental error socializes us to seek for and recognize quantities only. This applies to many areas of life – from aptitude, whereby we are only good at a certain subject if we have certain grades, to illness, where without certain blood test results we are not sick, to mental phenomena. With regard to the nature of the human being, mental phenomena are of particular interest – the modern human being tends to only consider that that which appears as *measurable* or *quantifiable* to consciousness is real. We can measure brain activity, we can measure electrical activity and neurotransmitters and so on, therefore, we consider that we have *explained* how these qualities (i.e. mental experiences) have come to be. This ingrained way of thinking, whereby the quantity is mistaken for the perception of quality, is alluded to in C.S. Lewis' popular Chronicles of Narnia, in the book *The Voyage of the Dawn Treader*. Eustace, a boy very much schooled in the modern scientific way of thought, meets a wise old man, Ramandu. Ramandu says to Eustace that in the land of Narnia stars are beings. Eustace interjects that 'in our world, a star is a huge ball of flaming gas', to which Ramandu replies: 'Even in your world, my son, that is not what a star is but only what it is made of' (Lewis, 2010b, p. 159).

In order to help clarify why these concepts are important, we shall briefly define three important terms alluded to previously – namely, quanta, qualia and phenomenology. In modern philosophy and psychology, *quanta* refer to measurable phenomena such as the objects of the external world. *Qualia* refer to the properties experienced by consciousness, such as feelings, thoughts and memories. The need for the distinction arises because an unsolved problem for neuropsychology and philosophy is how something physical such as the brain (i.e. a quanta) can produce something non-physical such as consciousness (i.e. qualia). With current physical measures, it is only possible to measure the neural correlates of qualia, not the qualia themselves. Thus, recognizing this problem, philosophy introduced the term *qualia* as a kind of unit of consciousness to go side by side with *quanta*, the units of matter.

Additionally, the school(s) of phenomenology basically argue that it is more often than not a mistake to separate phenomena into constituent parts: instead, the phenomena themselves need to be considered in their entirety (i.e. returning to Goethe, 'nothing is inside, nothing is outside'). For a phenomenologist, there is no justification in separating the qualia from the quanta – both belong to the very same phenomenon (i.e. 'for that which is inside is also outside'). Taking the example above, brain activity is the physical manifestation of a thought, as is the experience of the thought appearing in consciousness. Similarly, the idea of a tree is inseparable from the physical tree, and the nature of a person is difficult to separate from the manifestation of that person physically. As we discuss in later sections, this has vast implications for perceiving children (i.e. 'thus grasp without delay') because that which we can perceive often reveals something about their inner natures (i.e. 'the divine revealed openly').

Returning to the fundamental error that we make in this modern age when trying to understand what reality is, consider the following: We perceive a human being or a tree and then ask ourselves what a human being is, or what a tree is. Perhaps we also remember from our school education that the impressions that we take in through our eyes and other sense organs are really just caused by the vibrations and collisions of the external world with receptors in our eyes and skin, and so forth (see 4.4.1), which are then conveyed to our brain. We then generally believe that the brain, in some as-yet undiscovered way, spins up qualia (experience) from quanta (electrophysiological activity), but that qualia are just a subjective by-product of quanta, constructed by the brain. This is the materialist or atheist position, and also one that underlies much of modern philosophically constructivist education.

The materialist position is problematic in many regards. The most fundamental flaw is that the above line of reasoning provides no explanation for how the brain conjures up conscious experiences (qualia) from quanta. Secondly, this account just simply shifts experience from one place to another (Steiner, 1918/1986). Instead of seeing the qualia as existing in the environment (e.g. the beauty of a tree belongs to the tree), it is denied at its birthplace, because the tree is not really there because it is just a lump of molecules hardly distinguishable from the environment construed as a tree by our brains. The tree is denied existence in the sense organs, because in the latter, only electrical impulses are present (see Chapter 5); and it is also denied a place in the brain, because here only electrophysiological activity is present. The *experience* of the external world (of the tree, in this case) according to this constructivist position[2] is nowhere to be found and, as argued below, the question needs to be addressed as to what unique claim to reality quanta have, if everything is actually experienced as qualia.

Finally and most seriously, the above line of reasoning, although in the guise of a series of logical conceptual steps (if A, then B) actually contains a mixture of perception and (pre-)conception that often goes unnoticed. The line of reasoning is based on the hypothesis that qualia are caused by quanta, that the vibrations of small particles are the *same* as sound or light etc. Then, by treating quanta and qualia as synonymous, the argument tries to show that qualia do not exist as anything except constructions in our brains. The scientists themselves are usually very careful to formulate activity in the brain as a 'neural correlate' of experience, not as the experience itself. Somehow, however, this crucial distinction is lost: a careful line of scientific enquiry is used to support an idea that has strong consequences for society and education, because our very existence is reduced to some subjective by-product of quanta. Thus, all that is good and true in the world is relegated to mere subjective experience (Lewis, 2010a).

An alternative way of viewing this problem is to begin by asking, 'What is actually first experienced?' A close examination reveals that in the first place 'I' experience the world. Based on this experience, I then develop the above line of reasoning trying to prove that my experience is a product of quanta. This creates a logical paradox because the starting point is actually a *quality* – the starting point is consciousness. All quanta are first experienced as qualia, so why do we begin by assuming that the world is made of quanta and not qualia? Is it not less biased to say that I am first and foremost conscious, and only from this starting point do I discover that I also belong to a physical world?

In contrast to the materialistic view, the phenomenological view as described here maintains that the world consists of many qualia – colours, sounds, shapes, ideas, feelings, states of consciousness – that sometimes appear as quanta (the physical tree etc.); that is, in a form that presents itself quantifiably to consciousness. We then use properties of the world of qualia, such as logic, to investigate and derive quanta from the world. The experience of measuring, counting and weighing arises through our interacting with the objects and beings of this world in a particular and systematic way; however, in the words of Ramandu, it can only tell us what things are materially made of, not what they actually *are*. To really understand what something is, is only possible through the many different facets open to our conscious investigation, which includes, but is not restricted to, the objectively measurable physical world.

In this short section, we have taken the reader through a complex philosophical argument that leads us to the point, we believe, where we seriously need to examine alternative ideas of what the human being is. The starting point for doing this is, we think, phenomenology, the likes of which Goethe (the German equivalent of a mixture between Shakespeare and Leonardo da Vinci) advocated.

3.2 The threefoldedness of the human being

> Goethe's thoughts draw our attention to three different kinds of things: first, the objects we constantly receive information about through the gateways of our senses, the things we touch, taste, smell, hear and see; second, the impressions they make on us, which assume the character of liking or disliking, desire or disgust, by virtue of the fact that we react sympathetically to one thing and are repelled by another, or find one thing useful and another harmful; and third, the knowledge we 'quasi-divine beings' acquire about the objects as they tell us the secrets of what they are and how they work.
>
> *(Steiner, 1914/1994, pp. 22–23)*

The aim of the previous section was to draw attention to the impossibility of avoiding researching the qualitative, soul-spiritual side of our existence, because we experience the world first and foremost as a sum of qualities. However, what we experience as quantitative objective reality is also a part of our experience of this world, and must be taken seriously. Our aim is not to relegate the importance of science or objective measures of experience; we just seek to highlight the fact that although science relies on external measures, it is still the qualitative side of science (e.g. interpretation, understanding, mathematics, concepts, definitions) that manifests in awareness. Indeed, of crucial importance is that we learn to perceive these qualities with the same sharpness of mind that we perceive quantities, measure temperature, height, distance etc. This process of sharpening the mind lies at the heart of Steiner's anthroposophy.

Interestingly, casting a glance across the scientific disciplines reveals a threefold nature. Each discipline tends to concern itself with the one or other aspect.

Generally, the following sciences deal with the body: physics, chemistry, anatomy and neurology. Some disciplines are more directly concerned with the soul, namely psychology and sociology; and a few have begun to deal – although often indirectly – with the spirit: anthropology, philosophy and, in a sense, mathematics. However, according to a phenomenological view, these three aspects are really different sides of the same phenomenon, so none can really be viewed in isolation. In fact, the more one delves into a particular discipline, the more it tends to encroach upon other fields. Thus, education as a field has come to include physical sciences (e.g. neurophysiology), the science of the soul (e.g. psychology) and the spirit (e.g. philosophy).

This threefoldness was also noted by Aristotle (2003) in his discussion of ethics and the human being. Aristotle spoke of a *physis*, *psyche* and *nous* (Bischof, 2014), which corresponds well to *body*, *soul* and *spirit*. He also argued that qualities usually appeared in threes: cowardice was not the opposite of bravery, but these were related to each other in a threefold way with foolhardiness. In Christianity, the Trinity is threefold, comprising the Father, Son and the Holy Spirit; and in the writings of St Paul and Thomas Aquinas, a threefolding into body, soul and spirit was also spoken of.

Modern psychology, although not always recognized as such, speaks of a threefolding of the human being, with this comprising affect, behaviour and cognition, which have strong parallels to Steiner's idea of body, soul and spirit and also, as will be explained later, thinking, feeling and willing (3.4). In lay psychology, one often refers to people as 'thinkers', 'feelers' or 'doers'. Of particular interest is the development of this distinction within the 150 years of empirical psychology itself. Psyche in Greek (Ψυχή – psyche) means 'soul', and Sigmund Freud (although no longer as popular as he once was) was instrumental in developing the field of psychology with his insights and speculations on the nature of the human soul. The next development in mainstream psychology was a reaction to Freud and the focus of psychology on the 'science of behaviour'. In more recent times – in step with the development of the computer – the focus has shifted more to cognitive processes. That is, we can trace through psychology the changing focus on the different elements of the human being from the feeling or soul life, to the behaviour (with its physical correlates), over to cognition (as a function of the spirit) (see also section 2.2).

Only in recent years have there been attempts to unite these three into unitary, nigh-on phenomenological theories (e.g. in the field of embodied cognition) (Shapiro, 2011; Thelen, 2000). Although Steiner brought a greater degree of differentiation to each of these terms, these historical examples help to indicate that there is considerable justification to the idea that the human being is of a threefold nature.

3.3 The threefold human in anthroposophy

The previous section provides examples of how the threefold nature of human beings has been recognized in various domains of life; in this section we further develop this idea from the perspective of anthroposophy. In his book *Theosophy*, Steiner essentially carries out a detailed phenomenology of human existence. This phenomenology of the physical and psychological-intellectual led to his conception of the human being. He recognized three aspects of the human being, the first being the most obvious – namely, the physical body which belongs to the physical world. Secondly, he saw a second side of existence in which human conscious experience has its seat, and where the world is experienced and impressions received – this he called the 'soul'. Just as the physical body belongs to the world of matter, an experiential body belongs to a world of soul (or feeling).

Finally, Steiner recognized that there was a third aspect that is not transient and fleeting like the impressions of the soul, but that seeks to inscribe its own nature into the world of soul and physical substance; this he called the spirit. The following experience alludes to the three elements:

> Suppose I walk through a field where wildflowers are blooming. The flowers reveal their colors to me through my eyes – that is the fact I accept as given. When I then take pleasure in the wonderful display of colors, I am turning the fact into something that concerns me personally – that is, by means of my feelings, I relate the flowers to my own existence. A year later, when I go back to the same field, new flowers are there and they arouse new joy in me. The previous year's enjoyment rises up as a memory; it is present in me although the object that prompted it in the first place is gone. And yet the flowers I am now seeing are of the same species as last year's and have grown in accordance with the same laws. If I am familiar with this species and these laws, I will recognize them again in this year's flowers...
>
> *(Steiner 1914/1994, p. 23)*

Through our body and corresponding senses we are able to perceive the flowers, through our soul we experience the relevance of these for us in the form of feelings, and through the spirit we are able to recognize the permanence in the flowers. Again, the phenomena of the outer world serve as teachers of the inner, qualitative side. What can be recognized as laws of nature have their corresponding inner spiritual laws. Thus, the spiritual, such as in the laws of mathematics, lifts the human experience out of the purely sensual-experiential into something less transitory.

Briefly, this threefolding is not limited to that of body, soul (or psyche), and spirit (or mind), but each of these in turn also has a 'threefoldedness'. Thus, the body can be divided into three operative systems: namely, the limb-metabolic (muscular-skeletal), the rhythmic (breathing, heart rate) and the nerve-sense system (peripheral and central). The psyche, or soul, also has three different qualities that, somewhat simplified, comprise a feeling or sentient aspect, a thinking or reasoning part, and a self-conscious component. According to Steiner, the spirit or mind will also be increasingly differentiated into three parts in the further course of human evolution (ibid.). However, at the current phase of our development, the human spirit and 'I' are not really sufficiently ripe to be differentiated from one another, although there are differences.[3]

The human body reflects its physical nature most strongly in its limbs and metabolic system. In the rhythmic system, the soul is fairly strongly manifested in physical substance. For example, a feeling of excitement or guilt, which is a soul or psychological state, manifests strongly in alterations in heart rate, skin perspiration or breathing, for example. From a phenomenological point of view, this indicates a strong link between the rhythmic system and feeling. The spirit manifests in the nerves and senses because these are needed to perceive information in the outside world or in the body, to then process this information so that it can be consciously experienced as ideas. Of course, these systems are intertwined: the nerve-sense system is needed to perceive what is happening in the rhythmic system, or heart-rate changes can be observed when predominately thinking activity is taking place.

We tend to know a fair amount about our bodies and increasingly about our psychological make up, thanks to established disciplines and the perceptible nature of these two. In comparison, the spirit, or 'I', is more difficult to understand for several reasons. First, the 'I' is often confused with self-awareness, whereas here something more subtle is meant. Secondly, the 'I' cannot usually perceive itself directly, only via external reality (i.e. the body, the physical world); thus, we often confuse the workings of the 'I' for the 'I' itself, such as in the illusion that we feel our true selves to be our bodies. Thirdly, the 'I' is the most immature member of our being, such that its presence in cultural evolution is only beginning to really take effect. In other words, the 'I' works in a subtle way, making it less perceptible.

Generally speaking, the defining characteristic of the human spirit or 'I' is that it works to make what is transitory, permanent. For example, the 'I' seeks to overcome the processes of decay and decomposition in the physical world by imposing structure and order on the environment, by breaking down what is externally there so that something new can be built up according to its own laws. The 'I' seeks to add permanence to the fleeting, thus events are written into memory (body), fleeting feelings are raised into aesthetic experiences (soul), and a desire to understand and formulate laws (mind) arises. When the 'I' binds itself to the sentient part of the soul, feelings of beauty, awe or joy can replace those of mere attraction, fear or pleasure. When the 'I' binds itself to the part of the soul that is becoming self-conscious, then the desire to act with a social conscience arises, as can extreme individualism. With this description, we challenge the reader to consider this threefolding closely, to try and observe how it arises within oneself and particularly with regard to the education of the small child. Indeed, this threefold view of the human being has the potential to be one of the most fruitful contributions of anthroposophy, particularly in psychology, medicine and education.

3.4 Thinking, feeling and willing

In Steiner's later work in particular (Steiner, 1919/1996b), he approached his conception of the human being from yet another angle. He pointed to three foundational forces that characterize the human being's activity and nature – namely, thinking, feeling and willing. To understand these forces, it is important to see how, in his later work, Steiner moved from emphasizing the world in terms of what it is, to what forces were active in it. This change can be seen as shifting from the human being viewed as a spirit, a soul, a body, to the human being lives *in* thinking, feeling and willing. In this way, the universe is not static and abstract but instead exists through its constant evolving activity. This approach follows from Goethe and is potentially revolutionary, shifting the question from what there is to what is *becoming*.

From an educational point of view this brings a completely different and more constructive approach to viewing children. Instead of asking, say, what are a child's academic performance or physical capabilities like, we might ask what forces are active in the child, and what the child might become. There is less room for fixed judgements or appraisals (e.g. that a child is 'uncoordinated' or 'unintelligent'), and more consideration of where a child's strengths or weaknesses currently lie. This sets the child free from prejudice and static judgements, and allows her or him a role in shaping future development.

To really be able to grasp this picture of the human being and develop educational implications from it, a deeper phenomenological analysis of thinking, feeling and willing might prove helpful. First, we are far more conscious of our thoughts than we are of our feelings and, in turn, of our willing. In thinking, an overview of every step is possible; when trying to solve a logical problem, I exclude and include, sort and order each of my thoughts. In stark contrast, in willing we are only really conscious of the intention to act; intention is, however, a thought that seeks to connect itself with willing. We do not consciously guide one limb in front of the other while walking, we do not consciously direct our fingers into the right position when picking up an object; this happens automatically. In feeling, according to Steiner, we have a kind of 'dream' consciousness in contrast to a waking one for our thinking, and a deep sleep consciousness for our willing. As explained later, this largely unconscious nature of the will has important educational implications because children live strongly in this element (see section 5.2).

Another feature is that the present determines our relationship to the past and the future. Because the feeling concerns the present, we can say more precisely that feeling determines our relationship to the past and future. Feeling itself has two basic properties, according to Steiner, which he called sympathy and antipathy (Steiner, 1999). Sympathy refers to feeling attracted by, or having an interest in, something; antipathy is the opposite. Steiner argued that sympathy leads us to action, to doing something which, when connected to the will, leads to our future. Antipathy, in contrast, is a necessary prerequisite to objective thought because it allows us to distance ourselves from whatever it is that we are thinking about in order to then examine it properly. We know from conversations that if we feel sympathy towards the other person, we are more likely to believe what they say, whereas if we feel less positively, we bring our critical thought more to the foreground. This is one reason why social media, with their like/dislike judgements, are both popular and dangerous – they reduce the world to the realm of feeling (sympathy/antipathy), and actively bypass thinking and willing!

Continuing the analysis, we can also say that thoughts arise from the past, feelings from the present, and willing from the future. Beginning with feeling, we generally feel in response to immediate presences in the environment or in our body (e.g. hunger, fatigue, beauty). In contrast, our thoughts always deal with the past – that is, one's thoughts always concern something that we have first understood. Even thoughts about the future are based on our knowledge of past events and processes. To really illustrate the point, in the moment that we are thinking, for example about an apple, it is possible that the object relating to the thought 'apple' no longer even exists in the same form that it did when we began thinking about it (e.g. the apple may have been eaten, become riper etc.). In contrast our willing is always stepping into the future (e.g. 'I will...' when talking about the future).

The will is perhaps the most difficult to understand – yet because of the important role it plays in early childhood education, perhaps the most essential to comprehend. The easiest way to think of it is by analogy to the term 'will power'. In philosophy, the will is typically seen as the binding link between intention and action. For example, if we form the intention to prepare a drink, it is the will that turns this intention into action, and actually leads to us getting up and performing the action. Experientially, we all have times when we are more conscious of our will, particularly when it seems weakened (e.g. through exhaustion). Another example is attempting to change a long-held habit that has become second nature – here, extreme forces of will are required.[4] This provides another hint towards the importance of educating the will in the first phases of life, because this becomes much harder later on in life.

Another feature of willing that has strong educational implications is that willing is 'fired up' and set into motion by sympathy. This sympathy then leads us to perform a new act out of a desire, leading us into the future (Steiner, 1919/1996b). Often, we do not realise at the beginning of a task just how much work it will be, such that if we knew this, we would never undertake the task in the first place; but somehow, we find the strength. If an educator wants children to behave in a certain way, such as set the table for lunch, the will

needs to be activated. The educator has two desirable options: either he or she creates a relationship to the child so that the child feels sympathy for the adult and performs, through imitation, the actions of the adult. Alternatively, the educator can make the activity appealing, so that the will is activated by the sympathetic connection to the activity itself. In contrast, appealing to rational explanations, or brandishing threats, is very ineffective or even harmful for small children.

Will seems to have disappeared from modern conceptions of education because it has not been possible to 'find' the will: it seems to work, but is not 'present'. Steiner described it thus:

> For normal consciousness the will is extremely baffling. It is the nemesis of psychologists simply because they view the will as something very real, but basically without true content. If you look at the content psychologists ascribe to the will, you will find this content always derives from thinking. Considered alone, the will has no actual content. It is also the case that no definitions exist for willing; to define the will is even more difficult because it has no real content.
>
> *(Steiner, 1919/1993, p. 52)*

According to Steiner, the will has several characteristic features. First, the will is that which draws us to what we are becoming, thereby being, by nature, in flux. In young children this is particularly evident when, for example, watching a child lift its head or roll over for the first time. The child does not know cognitively at this point that doing so will lead it, through a series of motor refinements, to advanced psychomotor activities, but nonetheless puts itself to such trouble because it is driven on by some force of will. The same applies to a greater or lesser extent to all milestones in early childhood (see section 5.2).

Secondly, the will works on us in a largely unconscious way. Here, we see the parallels between the philosophical definition of will and Steiner's conception: the will provides the connection between our intention or images and our carrying out those images in future behaviour. Given that the will is essentially the future of children because it is in the process of becoming, one could say that the will must be educated to give children their futures. It follows that in a certain sense, activities that deny the opportunity to develop will (e.g. watching television instead of being physically active) deny children their futures. Later, we look at how one goes about educating the will (see Chapter 6). Again, it is also interesting how the English language betrays this future orientation of the will in that we express future tense with the verb 'will' (e.g. we 'will' write this book tomorrow).

The will is difficult to understand because it is difficult to perceive and requires careful phenomenological examination. The philosopher and cognitive psychologist Gallagher writes about a concept he terms 'body schema', which is quite close to the understanding of the will outlined here. Gallagher describes body schema as the ability to do things with the body, even when awareness is absent (Gallagher, 2006), such as accurate reaching for objects without being able to see them (blindsight) and the impairment that results when the 'willing senses' (see section 4.2) are inactive.

Understanding the forces of thinking, feeling and willing gives rise to powerful educational impulses, which we outline in detail in later sections of this book (see Chapter 5). However, the first step to guiding and unfurling these forces involves being able to lead and direct them – which requires perception, and a functioning sensory organism. We therefore devote the next chapter to the human senses, as understood by Steiner and augmented with recent insight from scientific research.

In a Nutshell

- To understand human existence, phenomenology is needed alongside conventional disciplines.

- This phenomenological approach leads to viewing the human being as comprising mental (spiritual), psychological (soul) and physical (body) aspects.

- Philosophy that ignores the spiritual, soul and physical aspects can fall into one- or two-sidedness.

- The human being engages in three main types of activity: thinking, feeling and willing. All of these need to be educated if the experience is to be holistic.

CHAPTER 4

The Twelve Senses

> This is the first chapter of anthroposophy: the true nature and
> essence of our senses.
>
> *(Rudolf Steiner, Berlin, 23 October 1909)*

In educational discussions, the focus of early childhood education is often placed on intellectual and academic development (House, 2011). Intellectual and academic skills and knowledge are vitally important, but are these best mastered by beginning to train them in early childhood? If early learning is not laden with intellectual learning, then what should children do instead at this life stage that best capitalizes on their enormous learning flexibility and potential?

To answer this question, we will first introduce and describe the role that our senses play in our thinking or cognitive development. In recent times, a seismic shift has been underway in which modern cognitive scientists are beginning to think that thought and language are internalized sense experiences (Barsalou, 2008; Lakoff and Johnson, 2010; Zwaan and Taylor, 2006). Indeed, the senses take that which seems inanimate and lifeless and raise it to part of animate, living human experience (Sheets-Johnstone, 2010). If this were true, then it would follow that the aim of early childhood is not teaching academic skills, but first training the senses and the body. In this chapter we outline what senses are, and which senses we have.

4.1 The philosophical foundations of the human senses

Philosophers, physicians, physicists, psychologists, priests, phenomenologists and lay people have all grappled with the nature of our senses. To what extent can the senses be trusted, to what extent do the senses convey to us the true nature of the outside world, and what senses do we actually possess? Can we experience things that are not bound to the senses? If the senses do provide us with direct access to reality, then sensory experience would seem a good starting point for education – but do they?

One of the most widely believed ideas is that the senses are merely subjective. If we take hearing as an example, the conventional understanding runs like this: a piece of metal is struck and begins to resonate, which then sends its energy via vibrations in air particles that cause the ear-drum to vibrate. The vibrations of the ear-drum are transmuted into an electrical signal that is carried along the auditory nerve into the central nervous system, which is subsequently further processed by various auditory centres in the brain and is somehow transmitted into conscious experience. This line of observation has led many to believe that the human experience of sound is merely a construction of the auditory system. Sound is really only vibrations, so our brain must trick us into constructing the experience of sound when really all there is 'out there' are vibrations. Therefore, senses are physiological and arbitrary whims, making them, according to this thinking, organs of deception.

Carrying this line of thinking through to its conclusion, we would then have to see that everything appearing to us in the sense world is in reality subjective and not necessarily important in and of itself. It may not even exist but is really a property of some virtual reality conjured up by our brains in response to mere vibrations of particles. Many phenomena of this world (new life, spring flowers, art) are no more or less beautiful, inherently good, and true as any others (e.g. murder, destruction etc.). All are simply abstractions and properties of the individual brain and its ability to confabulate experiences, perceptions, thoughts and feelings. In his lectures on education, C.S. Lewis went so far as to argue that education steeped in this idea leads to the abolition of mankind (Lewis, 2010a). How can we educate children if the entire world is a subjective reality, devoid of any good, truth and beauty?

Other thinkers from Goethe to Mearleu-Ponty, however, afford the senses a central role. This is, at least for Goethe, in stark contrast to the constructivist view described earlier (see section 3.1) because the senses are given a role in showing us both a physical (quantitative) and an experiential (qualitative, soul-spiritual) side to phenomena. In other words, the physical 'vibrations' and 'electrical signals' are just the physical manifestation of the broader phenomena that we perceive with the help of the senses. A phenomenon such as Beethoven's ninth symphony requires many vehicles to exist – the written composition, the composer, musicians, instruments, time and space – but neither of these alone is Beethoven's ninth. The symphony has an existence that is both physical and non-physical, that extends beyond time and space and individual people. It would be ridiculous to say that Beethoven's symphony was just vibrations of air in a concert hall in Austria over 200 years ago!

Steiner himself referred to this phenomenological idea many times, in that everything spiritual requires a physical carrier (Steiner, 1909/1996a). If we follow this shift in thinking, then a new world opens up to us in which sensory experiences are given full value as true educators of reality both hidden and manifest, even as sculptors of the developing body. Each sensory modality can teach us something unique about the world and reveal its many phenomena in a unique way. So what sensory channels are available to us?

In modern language usage, to say that someone has a 'sixth sense' often raises sceptical, or at any rate curious, glances. Due to the widespread cliché or dogma that human beings have only five senses, Waldorf educators have often been confronted with a variety of reactions in asserting Steiner's claim that the human being has more than double the number of commonly accepted senses, namely twelve! Dating back to Aristotle, conventional wisdom recognizes the visual (seeing), auditory (hearing), tactile (touching), gustatory (tasting) and olfactory (smelling) senses. In addition, in Steiner education – and increasingly also in modern empirical and phenomenological research – a further seven senses are recognized: vestibular (balance), thermoception (warmth), interoception or proprioception (movement and position of one's own body in space), visceroception (health), phonetic/sound perception (language sense), thoughts/concepts, and a sense for the 'other' as an individuality ('I' sense). Before considering these senses in more detail, let us briefly discuss what senses actually are.

4.1.1 What is a sense?

Clearly there is some disagreement around the exact number of senses. Why is this? To better understand why, we need to first consider what a sense actually is, which requires us to return to the terms qualia and quanta (see section 3.1). To recap, the term quanta refers to countable, physical and measurable phenomena such as volume, temperature or number. Qualia refer to the experience of phenomena – thus the feeling of warmth, the impression of blue, or the aesthetic experience of listening to Beethoven's ninth symphony.

Definitions of senses typically involve several criteria. The first is that the experience be automatic, without the need for conscious analytical thought. We see 'red' and experience 'redness' directly, or smell 'sweetness' without the need for intermediary consideration. Of course, analytical thought can be applied after the fact (e.g. to decide whether the red was more of a yellow-red or a blue-red), but this comes subsequent to the immediate impression, and is usually exclusive to the analysis of sensory impressions. Thus, senses provide information or qualities directly to consciousness without the need for higher thought and judgement.

Secondly, senses deliver qualities (qualia) to consciousness, such as the impression of 'redness' or 'sweetness'. An historical example of this is found in the dispute between Goethe and Isaac Newton. Upon shining light through a prism, a spectrum is obtained with colours appearing that are red, orange, yellow, green, blue, indigo and violet. Newton thought that light was hence divisible into these colours; in other words, he thought quantitatively about what he perceived: red + orange + yellow + blue + violet = white light. Goethe rejected this view for a number of reasons, one of which being that light is a quality and cannot be divided, only quantities were divisible. For him, Newton made a fundamental error because he treated qualia like quanta. By virtue of their ability to convey qualia directly to human consciousness, senses have a unique role in influencing the development of thought, language, behaviour, emotions and dreams – in short, human experience in its entirety.

Thirdly, a criterion in determining the existence of a sensory channel is that it provides information that is qualitatively discrete from another sense. Visual information is unique from auditory information, in that both sources can exist independently from one another. One can feel nauseous (visceroception) while viewing a beautiful landscape, one can watch a drummer perform while processing the movements of one's own body (e.g. proprioception, by walking). Of course, it is possible that sensory channels interfere with one another, but this occurs at a level beyond immediate sensory input, at the level of sensory integration (see section 5.3.5).

A fourth criterion is that the senses relate to information embedded in the physical world. Thus, mind reading or predicting the future, if reliably possible, would not be a physical sense as currently being presented, but would be a super-sensible sense ('super' meaning 'above' – thus, above the sense world). At its most basal level, a sense says 'something is there, in the moment, that can be physically detected': that is, the eye says 'something is visually present', and the ear determines 'there is sound'. Initially, senses simply say, for example, whether colour/warmth/sound/language is being perceived by the observer.

Finally, there should be an accompanying physiological organ, or as we propose, this can also take the form of a sensory network (as in speech perception) that is responsible for the sensory processing. Thus, a physical organ or sensory system conveys information about a world experienced as existing outside of consciousness. This outside world can be either from the surrounding environment (e.g. vision) or within the person's own body (e.g. proprioception).

4.1.2 Counting the senses

From this characterization of the senses, it is clear that several aspects define what we call a sense, which has perhaps given rise to disagreement and ambiguity as to what our senses actually are. For example, if precedence is placed on the physical organs present coupled with what provides overt stimulation to our consciousness, then hearing, seeing, smelling, tasting and touching are the most obviously discernible, hence giving rise to the idea that we have only five senses. Based on the idea that the 'skin' as such is a sense organ, it is also understandable that life functions (visceroception), warmth (thermoception) and even movement of the limbs (proprioception) were often lumped together as 'touch'. In a similar vein, the proximity of the balance organ in the inner ear to the hearing sense has perhaps occluded seeing balance and hearing as separate senses.

As this description makes clear, in terms of discovering and researching the senses, there is no exact and single scientific method or discipline that suffices. Because experience is always important in defining a sense, the question cannot be left to physiology or neurobiology alone, but requires input from psychology (the science of the psyche or soul), physics and philosophy. In addition to these branches of science, the next sections consider how contributions from anthroposophy can further enrich our understanding of what senses are, particularly as Steiner's pioneering observations were made approximately 100 years ago when very few authorities considered the human being to have more than five senses.

From the perspective of anthroposophy, the senses can be approximately ordered according to three categories, sometimes called lower, middle and upper senses, or at other times known as willing, feeling and thinking senses. In a similar vein, a distinction is often made in sensory physiology and psychology between intero and extero senses (Trousselard et al., 2004), which is similar to that employed by Steiner for the willing and feeling senses, respectively. In reality, any such ordering is only indicative, however, and not perfect, because senses often combine to provide information, and senses are seldom exclusively operant in internal or external domains.

4.2 Lower, internal or 'willing' senses

The first category of senses is essentially concerned with the perception of one's own body, its location in physical space (vestibular and proprioception), relation to external objects (tactile) and its own state (visceroception). However, according to Steiner these senses also lay the foundation for the higher senses

– for example, the sense of touch is crucial for perceiving others. Further, these senses also tend to work together; thus, perceiving the effects of gravity can involve visceral, tactile and vestibular information (ibid.). In describing these senses, we attempt to first present something of the physiological basis, alongside a phenomenological analysis of the latter. In some instances there are illnesses or conditions that typify the senses, such that, where available, we also refer to such phenomena.

4.2.1 Sense of touch (tactile)

> It is perhaps the last time,
> That in my hand yours does rest,
> So near is your blood to mine,
> Oh were you only to know my distress.
> *(Christian Morgenstern, authors' translation)*[5]

The sense of touch, the tactile sense, was placed by Steiner as the first sense in his conception of the twelve senses. At a physiological level, the sense of touch comprises a series of fibres (slowly vs rapidly adapting, punctuate vs diffuse) that connect to four types of (mechano)receptors under the surface of the skin. Each of these four mechanoreceptors has a different shape and serves a different function: Meissner corpuscles for short contacts with the skin; Merkel disks for steady pressure of small objects; Ruffini endings for steady pressure to the skin, including stretching; and Pacinian corpuscles for larger levels of gentle stimulation, such as blowing on the skin (Sekuler and Blake, 2002). Children are born with a larger number of touch receptors that thin out with increasing age (ibid.).

In addition to providing high-calibre and important information to the human being, the sense of touch is also intimately related to the development of self-awareness, according to Steiner. Through the sense of touch we learn about the boundaries between ourselves and the external world, where our organism ends and the external world begins. From a phenomenological point of view, the qualia, that is the impressions of the touched object, appear to flow inward from the surface of the skin (you can try this out!). In this way, touch conveys the quality of the outside world to the inner organism (Soesman, 2000).

Interestingly, Steiner thought that the touch sense was essential for perceiving not only objects but where the 'I' meets the outside world. Does this mean that when another person touches us, for example when shaking someone's hand or embracing another person, we gain an impression of another person through touch? Regarding the importance of human touch, research has shown that (human) tactile stimulation is essential for growth in both animals and humans, with reduced tactile interaction in infancy resulting in stunted growth and social-developmental difficulties (Sekuler and Blake, 2002).

4.2.2 Sense of well-being (visceroception)

> [T]he astonishing purity of pain, how it will not be mixed with any other sensation.
>
> *(Charles Baxter, American novelist)*

The sense of wellbeing, or visceral sense, is used for perceiving internal states, such as those corresponding to particular organs. This sense is little understood and probably covers a broad range of experiences, likely including pain, hunger, nausea, needing to use the toilet and fatigue. Visceroception is one of the more difficult senses to investigate because its receptors are internal and cannot easily be activated, and secondly, because sensory experiences usually arise during abnormal states (e.g. during sickness).

Fortunately, for our daily experience visceral information is usually only conveyed when an organ is in discomfort – otherwise we would be constantly bombarded with sensations from the multitude of organs that comprise the body. A combination of receptors is spread throughout the internal human body, including: (a) mechanoreceptors or 'stretch' receptors, measuring pressure in or on particular organs; (b) chemoreceptors, useful in detecting changes in blood oxygen; and (c) osmoreceptors, relating to water levels in the kidneys, for example (Mast, 2014). It is also important from an educational point of view to note that some children have difficulty knowing when they are tired, hungry, need to use the toilet or are ill. From this, we can assume that nurturing this sense and allowing it time to unfold is an important task of the educator.

4.2.3 Sense of own movement (proprioception)

> She has no words, and we lack words too. And society lacks words, and sympathy, for such states. The blind, at least, are treated with solicitude – we can imagine their state, and we treat them accordingly. But when Christina, painfully, clumsily, mounts a bus, she receives nothing but uncomprehending and angry snarls: 'What's wrong with you, lady? Are you blind – or blind-drunk?' What can she answer – 'I have no proprioception'?
>
> *(Sacks, 2015, p. 55)*

The body is able to sense its own motion and position in space, which in psychology is called proprioception and sometimes kinaesthesis (from the

Greek keinein and aesthesis, meaning 'movement' and 'sensation'). Henry Bastian, one of the first to investigate this sense, defines the sense thus: 'By means of this complex of sensory impression we are made acquainted with the position and movements of our limbs… by means of it the brain also derives much guidance in the performance of movement generally' (Han et al., 2016). All movements of the body probably require proprioceptive information to allow the meaningful detection and guidance of current and future body positions (Blanche et al., 2012).

There are a number of mechanoreceptors in the joints of the body that are thought to detect movement of the body's limbs (Han et al., 2016). Although the sense of movement (proprioception) was first proposed nearly 200 years ago by the Scotsman Charles Bell (1774–1842), it has remained little studied, although it has received more attention recently. For example, athletes have been shown to have higher proprioceptive abilities than non-athletes (Lin et al., 2006), and both sport and the likes of Tai Chi can improve proprioception in the elderly (Liu et al., 2012). Children's proprioceptive performance probably reaches that of adults around puberty (Kagerer and Clark, 2015) before beginning to decrease slightly with increasing age (Dunn et al., 2015).

Gallagher and Cole (1995) describe the fascinating case of a deafferented patient (IW), who lost his sense of proprioception and touch following an illness which destroyed key nerve fibres at the base of his neck. The following excerpt shows how crucial the sense of proprioception is for the will (see also section 3.4):

> IW has no proprioceptive function and no sense of touch below the neck. He is capable of movement and he experiences hot, cold, pain, and muscle fatigue, but he has no proprioceptive sense of posture or limb location. Prior to the neuropathy he had normal posture and was capable of normal movement. At the outset of the neuropathy IW's initial experience was of complete loss of control of posture and movement. He could not sit up or move his limbs in any controllable way. For the first three months, even with a visual perception of the location of his limbs, he could not control his movement. In the course of the following two years, while in a rehabilitation hospital, he gained sufficient motor control to feed himself, write, and walk. He went on to master everyday motor tasks of personal care, housekeeping, and those movements required to work in an office setting.
>
> *(ibid., p. 374)*

In Steiner education, the sense of proprioception is understood more broadly as a sense of movement, because we learn from the body's movement to perceive movement more generally. This movement is found not only in physical objects around us (e.g. a rolling ball) but also in states of soul, in life itself (e.g. 'things are moving quickly'). Soesman (2000), an anthroposophical doctor who worked on understanding the senses, points to the intimate link between movement and intention, in that we move somewhere to achieve a specific purpose of which only we are aware. For Soesman, the sense of movement then lies at the foundation of us being able to sense our place and destiny in life. This has parallels to the description of the will given earlier, and of movement being a willing sense, as being a force that is orientating or moving us into the future.

4.2.4 Sense of balance (vestibular)

> It is as though humankind resides between the centre of the Earth
> and the vaults of the heavens, between these two extremes. Her force
> and physical dignity result from her upright gait, which become like
> the very guarantors of this force and moral dignity.
>
> *(Humbert de Superville, 1827, p. 3,*
> *Dutch artist, authors' translation)[6]*

Not only Humbert de Superville but Steiner, too, attributed great significance to the human being having an upright gait, enabling us to balance the forces

of gravity with those of the heavens – thus being open to both, but not dominated by the one or the other. This gait, along with other abilities, we owe to our sense of balance. The vestibular sense organ comprises semi-circular canals in the inner ear that are receptive to movements of the head around three axes (Gallagher and Ferrè, 2018). When functioning, these organs are extremely sensitive to movements of the head and, thereby, to gravity and the upright orientation of the human gait, in conjunction with combinations coming from vision, proprioception and visceroception (Trousselard et al., 2004).

Taking a phenomenological view of the sense of balance, this sense receives a special and often understated role. Recent studies indicate that this vestibular sense is important for a number of functions that extend beyond physical balance. Thus, numerous studies show that the sense of balance is often disturbed in people suffering from anxiety (Saman et al, 2012): from a phenomenological point of view, it is interesting that anxiety and balance relate, and the English language alludes to this when 'life gets out of balance', or we feel emotionally 'imbalanced'. Additionally, impaired balance performance has been found in children diagnosed with Attention Deficit Hyperactivity Disorder (ADHD) (Shum and Pang, 2009), and in other learning disorders there are also hints that the sensorimotor system is affected (see section 5.3.8). By definition, a disorder represents dis-order or im-balance – hence, language again betrays a link that is born out in psycho-physiology.

4.3 Middle, mediatory, or 'feeling' senses

The next group of senses more directly involve the external world than the previous category, but still generally concern internal human experiences, so these are called the middle senses. Steiner also called these senses 'feeling' senses, because they most strongly speak to the feeling life. The senses belonging to this category are the sense of smell, taste, sight and warmth.

4.3.1 Sense of smell (olfaction)

> Smell is a potent wizard that transports you across thousands of
> miles and all the years you have lived. The odors of fruits waft me
> to my southern home, to my childhood frolics in the peach orchard.
> Other odors, instantaneous and fleeting, cause my heart to dilate
> joyously or contract with remembered grief. Even as I think of
> smells, my nose is full of scents that start awake sweet memories of
> summers gone and ripening fields far away.
>
> *(Helen Keller)*

The sense of smell is the first of what Steiner calls the feeling senses and, as evidenced in the above quotation from the both deaf and blind author, Helen Keller, a most potent and evocative wizard. Smell (and taste) are strongly feeling senses in that there is often an immediate link between smell and emotion; thus, in walking into an environment, a familiar smell often instantly recalls a specific experience, tagged to a powerful emotion, often from many years ago. The specificity and rapidity with which this kind of smell-memory happens is remarkable. Smell is also astoundingly sensitive; for example, people are more likely to correctly guess the gender of a person based on the smell of the other's palm or breath (Sekuler and Blake, 2002).

Perhaps the best evidence for Steiner's claim that smelling is a feeling sense arises from attempts to classify smells into dimensions, in the way that vision can be classified into colours. Such attempts have to date only resulted in one reliable universal classification of odours, across a spectrum from unpleasant to pleasant (ibid.). Thus, feelings, which according to Steiner are in their most primal form experienced as sympathy or antipathy (see section 3.4), are experienced similarly to odours. Anatomically, the nose contains sensory receptors which are transmitted via nerves to the olfactory bulb and then into the cerebral cortex (ibid.).

4.3.2 Sense of taste (gustation)

> To possess taste, one must have some soul.
> *(Marquis de Vauvenargues, 1715–1747)*

The sense of taste is, along with smell, clearly discernible as a feeling sense. The transformative effect of culinary experiences on mood has been noted times immortal, and the particular aesthetic experiences and relationship building around shared meal times is emphasized in just about every culture. The strong link between taste and the soul, or the feeling life, is therefore a powerful force of cohesion with an important role to play in education. As we discuss later, mealtimes are an important aesthetic experience shared in the kindergarten community (see Chapter 6), and the sense of taste can be cultivated through sound nutrition. Such measures, we argue, help cultivate our interaction with food, such that it remains a good servant and does not become our master. Finally, it is also important to emphasize how the sense of taste generalizes to soul experiences in general. People can be 'of good taste', perform 'distasteful' acts or have a 'tasteless' sense of humour.

Aristotle originally conceived of there being seven taste qualia – sweet, sour, salty, bitter, pungent, harsh and astringent. Across the course of time, this was simplified to four (i.e. sweet, salty, sour and bitter) and recently extended to five, with the addition of umami (Sekuler and Blake, 2002). Although influenced by the sense of smell too, the tongue operates as the main organ of taste, with many of its papillae containing taste buds, which are also found throughout the rough of the mouth and cheeks (ibid.). New-born infants have relatively few taste buds, with these increasing until around age 40, after which they start decreasing in number. There is also good evidence that early experiences have a long-lasting impression on taste preferences – hence the need to lay the foundations for healthy nutrition in the early years (see section 6.6).

4.3.3 Sense of sight (vision)

> Since colour occupies so important a place in the series of elementary
> phenomena, filling as it does the limited circle assigned to it with
> fullest variety, we shall not be surprised to find that its effects are
> at all times decided and significant, and that they are immediately
> associated with the emotions of the mind.
> *(Johann Wolfgang von Goethe, 1810/1840, p. 304)*

If we examine closely the sense input from sight, we actually only perceive colours through the physical eye: all object recognition is actually a recognition of ideas, concepts and constructs. If we focus intensely on colour, then emotional or aesthetic qualities come into the foreground. For example, according to Goethe 'in red is seeking and desiring; in yellow, finding and knowing; in white, possessing and enjoying' (Hensel, 1998, p. 79). The sense of sight can therefore primarily be seen as a feeling sense. In modern life, the

sense of sight has become an informational sense because we often spend many hours a day glued to computer screens, newspapers and books. However, as argued later in this chapter, here we are perceiving ideas and language that we lump together with the visual sense when reading (see section 4.4.3). As mentioned later, trying to remove the bias arising from conceptual influences and return to a child-like immediacy of visual experience is an interesting undertaking (section 5.3.7).

Anatomically, and psychologically, the sense of sight has probably received the most attention. Light passes through the lens of the eye, which flips the visual image upside down and projects this to the back of the eye (retina). The retina contains two types of photoreceptors (rods and cones), each 'tuned' to receive different wavelengths of light that correspond to different colours (Sekuler and Blake, 2002). The optic nerve, after crossing to the other side of the body, then carries signals from the eye to the visual cortex and beyond. Generally speaking, from the visual cortex (which is at the back of the brain), signals are then spread diffusely across the brain, depending on what is being perceived and processed.

Phenomenologically speaking, the sense of sight is remarkable in that it shows how strongly our concepts influence what we experience through sight. For example, the 'images' themselves are flipped upside down by the eye, crossed to the other side of the body, and then, after being sent right to the back of the brain, are spread right across the cortex. Despite this process of deconstruction we still experience our percepts as wholes. Furthermore, it is possible to wear glasses that flip the world upside down – however, fairly quickly, the visual system will automatically correct this and turn the world back the right way up (ibid.). Our eye also experiences many obstructions (e.g. floaters, blindspots, blinking), contains a large blind spot, and is colour blind in the periphery (ibid.), yet again we still experience the world as a visually coherent whole. This serves to demonstrate that the visual system, at least for adults, is heavily influenced by idea and concept, not merely by the variations in colour impressions actually perceived by the human eye. Seeing, as we experience it, is an intelligent and integrated process depending on other senses and conceptual seeing, to fill in the holes thrown up by our physical organs. Characteristic of this separation, patients who suffered from neurological damage can have trouble being aware of half of their visual field, although they can see it, or seeing objects for which they can accurately reach (Sacks, 2015).

4.3.4
Sense of warmth (thermoception)

> There lies the heat of summer
> On your cheek's lovely art:
> There lies the cold of winter
> Within your little heart.
>
> That will change, beloved,
> The end not as the start!
> Winter on your cheek then,
> Summer in your heart.
> *(Heinrich Heine)*[7]

The sense of warmth has had a troubled past, initially being grouped together with either the sense of touch or with the life sense, or even with emotions. From a phenomenological point of view, the sense of warmth allows us to learn to perceive, first, physical warmth and, secondly, emotional warmth. This majestic quality of warmth radiates and permeates other qualities – much like physical warmth does with physical substance. This quality of warmth, including its absence which is felt as the quality of 'coldness', is found in human relationships, in the environment and in works of art. Warmth therefore encompasses both a physical-physiological and a soul-spiritual dimension.

Anatomically, the sense of (physical) warmth is provided through a series of thermoreceptors on the surface of the skin (Fulkerson, 2014; Schepers and Ringkamp, 2009). Thermosensation, the ability to respond to changes in temperature, is – from an evolutionary perspective – one of the oldest senses, found in all organisms including bacteria and plants (Vriens et al., 2014). Interestingly, in Steiner's conception of spiritual human evolution, warmth was the first quality that existed (Steiner, 1925/1997). The quality of warmth also has a unique link to the human 'I' and the physical world. According to Steiner, the 'I' is at a stage of development that can be compared to a differentiated warmth organism: thus, when we really 'meet' another person, we often feel a sense of warmth (or coldness). Many children also have difficulty perceiving their own warmth and, hence, regulating their own body temperature. This, in combination with the importance of warmth for the human 'I' – and obvious medical grounds – is a reason why the warmth sense and quality of warmth need to be particularly nurtured in the early years.

4.4 The upper, social senses

In the next group of senses, Steiner is both a pioneer and controversial, because he proposed that humans possess (in addition to hearing) three upper senses that have not, to our knowledge, otherwise been proposed. In addition to the commonly accepted sense of hearing, these are the sense of language, thought, and of another person's 'I'. At the outset, we want to be clear that Steiner died before he was able to complete his ideas on the senses, particularly the upper senses. Although he lectured on the senses, his written work on these remained largely uncompleted (Steiner, 2009). Therefore, we wish to emphasize the preliminary nature of our considerations in this section, as we try to develop Steiner's ideas incorporating modern research.

Although ostensibly the upper senses are more advanced and less prominent in early childhood development, we go into depth on these senses for two main reasons. There are important parallels between the upper and lower senses – the 'I' sense is intimately connected to the sense of touch (e.g. perceiving boundaries). Understanding these links again fleshes out our understanding of children and ourselves. Teachers can also work consciously with the upper senses so as to more effectively educate children. Being aware of how ugly or trivial language usage, dishonesty or falsehood actively deceive, respectively, the speech, thought and 'I' senses is an important component of becoming a more reflective and effective teacher.

In typical everyday experience, we are used to perceiving sounds along with language and an accompanying internal state, such as an emotion or a thought. Accordingly, we may be prone to ascribe much to the auditory sense that is perhaps best ascribed to a different sense or process, such as the speech or thought senses. Hence, caution and careful observation are required to determine how the upper senses suggested by Steiner exist and operate.

4.4.1 Sense of sound (auditory)

> Listen, the flute laments
> And the cool fountains rustle,
> Golden the notes waft down.
> Quiet, quiet, let us listen!
> *(Clemens Brentano, in Forster, 1990)*

For Steiner, the sense of sound encompasses the mechanic components in what we call the auditory sense, but as with the other senses, a more qualitative and phenomenological analysis is also required. Thus, the conventional view is that sound travels in waves through the air, which then make contact with the air drum, and then these waves, via the middle ear and the cochlear, are translated into an electrical signal that is conveyed along the auditory nerve (Sekuler and Blake, 2002). This signal is then processed by, amongst other areas, the auditory cortex, and is then transmitted to diverse areas of the brain. At this point, it is assumed that a conscious experience of the sound then somehow arises; that is, from the air vibrations, an electrical signal is created from which the brain somehow constructs the sound. As mentioned earlier (section 4.1.1), if fully thought through, this idea is the same as saying that a piece of music, or a loud bang, does not really exist.

This position is philosophically problematic for many reasons, particularly because it does not account for how the vibrations of particles (quanta) turn into the experience of sound (qualia). In terms of the mechanics of sound, in his book on the twelve senses Soesman (2000) took a different view, arguing that the purpose of the auditory mechanism was to eradicate the quantitative aspect of sound, so that the quality of the sound could be perceived by consciousness. We would add to this in suggesting that the quality of the sound is present in the stimulus: all that the ear does is direct our attention to the fact that we are hearing something at a certain frequency, thereby providing our consciousness with the physical apparatus to perceive the sound qualia.

A phenomenological investigation of hearing is insightful. Steiner thought that the hearing sense conveyed information about the internal states of objects or beings in the external world. When a piece of wood is knocked, it can produce a hollow, empty sound, or a heavy muffled sound. The former can indicate that the wood is very dry, or perhaps even hollow, while the latter could suggest that the wood is soaked through with water. Alternatively, the sound could indicate something about the state of what is knocking against the wood – that this is dry, hollow, soft or filled with liquid. The whole object resonates when sound is produced (as is the case with many musical instruments), and the internal dynamics of this object are decisive in determining the sound produced.

Even in simple physical phenomena, it is clear that the hearing sense conveys something about the internal state of objects in the external world. Perhaps it is worth considering at this stage how impressive a developed human hearing sense can be. An orchestra can be playing and a human ear can isolate from the sound of the oboes, the violins or a cough in the background. A person can be cooking and hear an object fall, and fairly quickly decide which object the child had just dropped, and where this occurred, based solely on the sound that the object makes. Such a sophisticated sense of discrimination does not develop quickly, and it is perhaps clear just how much exploring and playing with different forms of objects is necessary for children to develop this ability.

However, sounds are not only produced from inanimate objects, but also from living beings. How, then, is a scream, a song or a word related to the hearing sense? This question is surprisingly difficult to answer because in the case of living beings, more than the resonant state of the internal composition of an object is transmitted! That is, when a child laughs, this noise does not result from the mechanical response of an adult trying to determine whether the child is hollow or full of fluid, but rather due to an internal emotional state. For this reason, hearing is at the gateway to the social senses, because sound takes something inner in another being and conveys it to our inner. In the senses to be considered next, we explore where the hearing sense stops, and where other senses begin to work.

4.4.2 Sense of speech (phonological perception)

> For last year's words belong to last year's language
> And next year's words await another voice.
> But, as the passage now presents no hindrance
> To the spirit unappeased and peregrine
> Between two worlds become much like each other,
> So I find words I never thought to speak
> In streets I never thought I should revisit
> When I left my body on a distant shore.
> *(T.S. Eliot, 'Little Gidding')*

As outlined earlier (section 4.3.3), in the course of our development we have synthesized sensory impressions with concepts and ideas – such that we seldom perceive what is actually in front of the eyes or ears. For example, most people looking at a table would say that they see lines and a rectangle, perhaps. However, there are no real lines present to the eye, there are simply different gradations of colour. The lines are an acquired abstraction that we automatically impose on our visual experiences, without even noticing it. Similarly, we do not hear a 'bang', a 'melody' or a sentence, but we detect sounds that we identify as one of these phenomena. In doing so, we often combine a range of percepts and experiences that then became automatically, and nigh on inextricably, bound. It is probably the case that one learns what a 'bang' is not merely by having heard a loud noise previously, but also by seeing two objects collide that produce a loud sound, followed by the associated feeling of juddering in one's stomach. Conscious thought then couples the idea of a collision with the experience, such that whenever a bang is heard, all of these experiences well up at once.

In a similar manner, when we hear a word we also associate certain meanings and ideas with that word, once we have sufficient experience in the language in which that word is spoken. However, the first step is to recognize that a language is being spoken at all; Steiner variously called this ability either the word, speech, or sometimes also the phoneme sense (Wortsinn, Sprachsinn or Lautsinn). Thus, just as hearing tells us 'there is sound', the word sense tells us that 'there is language'. Before we can perceive the qualities such as the ideas and personality that are being conveyed via speech, we must first know to direct our attention to the language (via the sense of hearing, but also gestures via vision in the case of deafness, or braille reading via touch in the case of blindness). Only once we know that what we are perceiving is language, Steiner thought, can we begin to grapple with its content, which requires the thought sense (section 4.4.3).

According to Steiner, the speech sense is a sense because it provides information directly to awareness without intermediary judgement being required (see section 4.1.1). This happens constantly and rapidly during the course of a conversation, such that we perceive that a conversation is occurring and can focus on it. If we had to constantly evaluate and judge whether speech was present, then we would not be able to attend to the thoughts in the speech.

Before turning to the thought sense, there are several aspects of speech development and disturbances that may shed light on the speech sense. There are neurological conditions in which patients cannot find the names for that which they wish to express (called Brocca's aphasia). These patients can describe an object in many ways but cannot find the word for the specific object. A similar condition experienced by almost everyone with increasing age, called anomia, refers to word-finding difficulty. One can search around for some time until one finds precisely the word that expresses the sentiment or thought. Presumably this represents the speech sense integrating, or tuning into, the thought.

It is also interesting to consider the development of language. Just as with the other senses, as addressed later in this book, this follows a timetable according to which experiences need to be provided, or language ability will be forever impoverished (see section 5.3.3). In the first months of life, infants are optimally able to acquire sensitivity to phonemes, discriminating among sounds across all languages – an ability that soon weakens (Polka et al., 2009). Moreover, children who are not exposed to the structure (grammar or syntax) of a language in the first years of life have more difficulty acquiring this at a later age. Mastering a second language becomes increasingly difficult after around the tenth year of life.

It remains unclear from Steiner's work how these different aspects of language relate to the speech sense. However, given that he alternated between the terms phoneme-sense, word-sense and speech-sense, and that these correspond to the three areas of language recognized by research (phonology, semantics and grammar), it is likely that these three aspects are to the speech sense what rods and cones are to the visual sense. In terms of neural processing, although having specific centres, speech is, much like vision, processed by a wide network of neural areas spread across the cortex (Huth et al., 2016).

4.4.3 Sense of thought

> Because speech – natural speech – does not consist of words alone, nor… 'propositions' alone. It consists of utterance – an uttering-forth of one's whole meaning with one's whole being – the understanding of which involves infinitely more than mere word-recognition.
>
> *(Sacks, 2015, p. 85)*

The sense of thought can be most simply understood as providing an answer to the question 'Is thought present?', before one begins to form judgements as to what the thoughts present might indicate. Returning to the example of vision, one first sees something with the eye, thus determining 'colour is visually present'; then in a second step we can recognize the object or source of the colour. In an analogous way, according to Steiner we first perceive the existence of a thought, and then we use our intellectual and perceptual faculties to understand or judge the thought: 'There is namely an immediate perception for that which is revealed in concepts, such that one has to also speak of a thought-sense' (Rudolf Steiner, 12 August 1916, authors' translation). Steiner maintained that this process of perceiving the presence of thoughts was automatic and rapid, such that it, too, fell into the category of being a sense, albeit an upper or higher sense.

The question of what a thought actually is, is surprisingly difficult to answer. Typically, one might answer that a thought is an idea – which is mere tautology – or that a thought is an experience caused by brain activity (a view which does not actually shed light on what a thought is). From a phenomenological point of view, just as sound waves physically indicate that 'sound is there', thoughts also have 'carriers'. Two possibilities exist that could be seen as the physical carriers of thoughts: one is the object of thought itself, and the second is the thinkers of the thoughts.

From the way that Steiner described the sense of thought, it seemed that he believed that this sense was active in perceiving and following the thoughts of someone who is speaking. In this case, the words of the speaker carry the thoughts, and the listener perceives or receives the thoughts. According to Soesman (2000), to clearly perceive a thought we need to shut out the auditory signal and remove the language perception, so that we can focus and 'live into' what the speaker is conveying. The following example might make this clearer. In a lecture where the speaker's accent or way of speaking is particularly striking, one often spends the first ten minutes or so 'listening to' the language and paying less attention to the content. Sooner or later, however, one becomes aware that one has stopped listening to the language or the way of speaking and has moved over to hearing, or perceiving, the thoughts of the speaker.

There is a clear, intimate connection between language and thought, such that some schools of philosophy go so far as to maintain that thoughts are the same as language, that language is the foundation of knowledge. Modern psychological work, however, tends to agree that thoughts can be clothed both as pictures and language (Sadoski and Paivio, 2013). However, this only says what form a thought takes, not what a thought actually is.

So, what is a thought? Plato experienced thoughts as being the real content of the world, and the physical objects as being poor copies, as physical manifestations (Plato, 2012). This is perhaps most easily understood in the realm of mathematics in that we use many mathematical concepts that are simply not found on Earth (e.g. negative numbers, infinity), or at best exist as poor copies of an ideal (e.g. a straight line and other geometric forms, sine waves, numbers themselves). Here, despite millennia of trying, there are seldom satisfactory answers to basic questions like 'What is a number?'. For Steiner, as argued in his book *The Philosophy of Freedom*, an idea belongs to the object, to the phenomenon, not to us.

Phenomenologically, any given 'thing' has many different levels of manifestation. Staying with the example of the tree (see section 3.1), a tree is many physical things (magnetic, solid, light-reflecting) and also many qualitative and physically invisible manifestations too (e.g. colour, shape, an aesthetic feeling), among which is the concept of the tree. Just as it would be absurd to say that the trunk or the greenness is not part of the tree, it is absurd to say that the thought 'tree' does not belong to the tree.

So what is a thought? We suggest that it is an aspect of reality that appears in thought form to the (thinking) mind. Thus, thoughts exist in nature, in people's minds, in worlds of idea (e.g. logic, counterfactual thinking) and these can be discovered – or uncovered – by this thinking mind, and perceived via the sense of thought.

For the other senses, a particular organ or network of nerves has been found. Remembering that Steiner also conceived of these twelve senses as providing information derived from the physical/quantitative world, a question arises as to where the organ for a thought-sense might be located. This is clearly a complicated problem, and given that the thought sense is not currently recognized as such, there have been no direct scientific investigations into this issue. However, in the interests of stimulating the readers' thoughts and further inquiry, here are some suggestions.

First of all, there is the idea of embodied cognition (see Lakoff and Johnson, 2010; Shapiro, 2011), which is becoming a popular idea in philosophy, cognitive science, education, linguistics and computer science. The basic premise of embodied cognition is that thinking does not occur in some specific corner of the brain, but instead involves the periphery of the body (Barsalou, 2010). Some argue further that the thought is inseparable from not only the body but also the environment; these all are part of the same complex dynamic system (Lakoff and Johnson, 2010; Thelen, 2000).[8] Findings from neuropsychology and cognitive science indicate that for many kinds of thoughts, motor skills and actions are involved (Suggate and Stoeger, 2017; Zwaan and Taylor, 2006). When participants process words that are related to the concept 'arm' or 'leg' (e.g. shoe, run, throw), the corresponding motor area of the participants' brains is activated (Pulvermuller, 2005; Pulvermuller et al., 2001). Other theorists view thought as a re-imaging of sensory experience (Kosslyn et al., 1990). Taken together, it seems that thinking involves the whole body, because this is a re-perceiving of that which was previously experienced with the lower and middle senses.

So where, then, is the organ for the sense of thought? There appears to be no specific region of the brain that is responsible for thinking; instead, many different regions are involved for different kinds of thoughts. As such, we suggest that different regions of the brain and possibly the peripheral nervous system are involved in perceiving thoughts, depending on which bodily or idealistic experiences lie at the foundation of the given thought.

Finally, it is interesting to consider two forms of disability – first autism, and secondly William's syndrome. Autism will be dealt with in more depth in the next section, but it needs to be mentioned here because in some respects, autism spectrum disorder and William's syndrome seem to be opposite conditions. Some people with autism spectrum disorder have difficulty relating to other people, but can be high functioning, sometimes with excellent speech (American Psychiatric Association, 2009). People with William's syndrome, in contrast, have very low cognitive functioning but intact speech – in fact, they are often described as socially benevolent and very conversational; but their cognitive functioning, and presumably also their thought sense, seems heavily impaired (Tager-Flusberg, 2009). Perhaps people with William's syndrome tend to have a weaker thought-sense compared to their speech and sense of 'I', whereas those with autism can have a good thought sense, with deficits in the sense of 'I' and, in the case of some forms of autism, of speech? To complete this picture, we now present the sense of 'I'.

4.4.4 Sense of 'I'

> A yet more intimate relationship to the external world than that provided by the thought-sense is given by the sense that enables us, in relation to another being, to perceive, to know, that it feels just as we do.
>
> *(Steiner, 12 August 1916, authors' translation)*

To understand the importance of the I-sense for human experience, as suggested by Steiner, one can consider the following thought experiment – although it is probably not long until the following becomes reality. Imagine the development of a computer program that can converse with you like a friend. Would you find it to be a worthy enterprise, after arriving home from work to an otherwise empty house, to tell this computer jokes, which are then rewarded by a computer laugh, however convincing? Would you confide your problems in the computer and feel better when it told you that your life really wasn't so bad, or that you looked nice in that dress, or were in good shape for your age?

Just as the visual sense tells us that something visible is there, the thought sense that thoughts are there, the I-sense tells us that another person is there. Steiner even suggested that our language is missing a verb for this: just as we have the infinitive verbs 'to hear' and 'to see' (in German, *sehen*, *hören*), we also need 'to I' or 'to ego' (something like: *ichen* in German, with the word '*ich*' turned into a verb) (Steiner, 1919/1993). He directly challenged the idea that when perceiving a person, we infer their presence and very existence based on external cues, that because someone is talking or waving his or her hand there must be a person there. For Steiner, there was a direct process of perceiving an individuality that precedes inference or judgement (Steiner, 1917/1996). Just as the thought-sense is not for perceiving one's own thoughts but those that one experiences in the environment, an I-sense is not the sense for one's own self, but for those in one's environment.

Steiner describes the I-sense as comprising a rapidly interchanging, almost oscillating process of sympathy and antipathy towards another person (Steiner, 1919/1993). In his words, one 'goes to sleep in the other person' (sympathy), then 'wakes up' and draws back. This process repeats itself continuously and rapidly such that it is unconscious.[9] One can almost imagine wave-like forms of sympathy at the peaks and antipathy at the troughs being received by the I-sense, similar to how waves of sound might work on the ear. If one observes human interaction closely, it is often possible to see a similar but more enduring interchanging: when there is too much sympathy towards the listener, it is as if a certain discrimination is missing; when there is too much antipathy, the impression is created that the person is not being perceived. If these two activities were imagined to rapidly oscillate, then Steiner's description of this mechanism seems conceivable.

Recent research provides fascinating insight into what appears to be key for the I-sense. Perception-action circuits have been proposed to exist, which are active when we perceive the actions of others or if we are performing those actions ourselves (Decety and Meyer, 2008). Although our limbs and muscles may appear still when watching another person, a kind of internal mimicry results that is played out in our brains and physiology (ibid.). These perception-action circuits are linked to the so-called mirror neuron system (Gallese, 2013), and may provide the physiological basis for perceiving intentionality in humans and animals (Carr et al., 2003).

The discovery of perception-action circuits and mirror neurons lead Gallese, one of the pioneering scientists who helped discover the existence of mirror neurons, to interesting insight on how we perceive others. Gallese's insights are very close to Steiner's conception of the I-sense:

> At the basis of the human capacity to understand others' intentional behaviour… there is a more direct access to the world of the other. Such direct access is made possible by the fact that human beings, like nonhuman primates, are endowed with [being able to] share the meaning of actions, basic motor intentions, feelings, and emotions with others, thus grounding the identification with and connectedness to others.
>
> *(Gallese, 2013, pp. 244–245)*

Like Steiner, Gallese sees the necessity in a 'direct access' to another human being and that this perception does not occur via 'attribut[ing] mental states to others' (ibid., p. 244). In other words, both Gallese and Steiner argue that the 'mainstream' view is incorrect – in Steiner's words, there must be a sense of others. Fascinatingly, both Steiner and Gallese were born 100 years apart and from vastly different scientific fields, and yet both come to a similar conclusion.

Research on empathy also sheds light on the 'I' sense, because to empathize with another, one has to be able to first perceive the other is there. Empathy is defined in different ways, but usually involves the ability to share in others' internal worlds (Walter, 2012). Research indicates that a complex perceptual system lies at the foundation of empathy. It appears that when feeling empathy, we first internally 'imitate' the person whom we are observing (Carr et al., 2003); and if his or her face is contorted in agony, then we internally 'contort' our face, measurable by activation of the corresponding areas of the brain (e.g. motor cortex). Empathic individuals show greater non-conscious mimicry of the facial expressions of others (ibid.). It seems that this research into empathy is also consistent with the presence of an I-sense, and perhaps also that empathy may 'fine-tune' the I-sense – with individuals who do not develop this ability socially blunting themselves to the worlds of others (Molnar-Szakacs, 2011). Earlier we alluded to two conditions, autism spectrum disorder and William's syndrome. It is again very interesting that social skills and empathy are hallmarks of both conditions, under-developed in autism and strongly developed in William's syndrome. Might autism be characteristic for what happens when the I-sense is deaf?

Just as light needs to work on the receptors of the eye for vision to develop, we believe that so too do human 'I's' need to work on our own 'I' sense so that this can develop. Educationally, because authenticity is indicative of the work of another 'I', it is therefore vital that children are given genuine experiences with other human beings, in order to develop both empathy and their I-senses. The increasing technology in the world, however 'user-friendly', would seem to be a poor substitute for genuine human experiences and interactions. Although more research is needed, the ramifications for education – including early education – arising from the existence of an 'I' sense are potentially enormous.

In the next chapter, we outline some developmental principles of the senses after first introducing the development of the child in a broader sense.

In a Nutshell

- Through our senses we are linked to the world, so understanding the human senses is the first step to understanding humanness.

- Senses reveal qualities of the outside world that are not mere subjective illusions.

- A phenomenological and psychological-physiological analysis of the human being reveals twelve human senses.

- Lower or body senses provide information about touch, health, movement and balance.

- Middle or feeling senses perceive smells, tastes, sight and warmth.

- Upper or social senses are tuned to sound, speech, thought and other individualities.

CHAPTER 5

The Development of the Child

In the twentieth century, the course of child development was a hotly debated and scientifically fruitful topic. Alongside Steiner's detailed descriptions of child development, which have not explicitly penetrated into the mainstream, other prominent theorists include Maria Montessori, Sigmund Freud, Jean Piaget, Lev Vygotsky, and in a sense also Burrhus Skinner.

Generally speaking, the advent and dominance of time-intensive empirical psychological and neurobiological research has taken the focus away from individual theorists to an accumulated body of systematic observations and experiments. Indeed, the literature is now so specific to individual aspects of child development that few researchers any longer think about or publish broader theories. Even one specific aspect of child development, say memory or language development, constitutes a broad field with multiple sub-disciplines and specialities such that it is nearly impossible for one researcher to have a deep overview of memory research alone. This is understandable, and even necessary, but brings with it the danger that we believe that specific details supplant the need for broader theories; in reality, both are required. For this reason, we first present an overview of the study of child development before turning to Steiner's ideas on the subject.

5.1 Quantitative and qualitative views of child development

For true education recognizes the whole human being to be educated. The debate and debacle of 'theories of education, learning, thinking, information processing, and systems of information retrieval' are relevant to computer programing [sic], not the education of human beings. What we need to realize is that the human being and mechanically derived systems meant to describe

the human being are not even remotely the same thing.
(Sardello and Sanders, 1999, pp. 244–245)

Again weaving its way through this book is the observation that the human being can be considered from a qualitative and a quantitative point of view. Qualitative views see childhood as being fundamentally different to adulthood, typified in the saying 'Children are not mini-adults'. Freud believed that children developed in stages, so-called psychosexual phases, each having its own unique character and accompanying needs. Montessori and Piaget also viewed childhood as passing through a series of qualitatively distinct phases, although Montessori was perhaps a bit more individualistic with regard to how children passed through these phases (Edwards, 2007). Piaget thought that children began life in a sensorimotor phase of development, passing through several phases into a stage where abstract thought was possible, at around puberty (Berk, 2004). In short, qualitative models see a series of unique, distinct and sequential phases of child development.

In contrast, quantitative views see children as being fundamentally similar to adults, with development occurring due to an increase in 'more of the same'. As the desire to measure change has intensified across the last decades, so too has the prevalence of quantitative views of development. Given that 'measurable' is a synonym for 'quantitative', it is not surprising that the mainstream view has become increasingly quantitative. However, a second reason for the dominance of quantitative views is a reaction against the speculative introspection present in the psychology discipline's early days.

B.F. Skinner, one of the fathers of behaviourism, believed that all knowledge and skill was conveyed through reinforcement and punishment of behaviour. Reinforcement and punishment are not referred to in the usual sense of the words, but rather indicate any environmental response that either increases or decreases the likelihood of a behaviour – a smile can be a reward, a frown a punishment. Skinner was fundamentally sceptical about anything to do with feelings or thoughts; for him these could not be measured so they should not be studied. He pushed them into a black box, and set about studying the effect of stimuli on behaviour.

Some time after Skinner's and the behaviourists' core work, the so-called 'cognitive revolution' occurred. This was based on the development of the computer, which came to be seen as a metaphor for human thinking. Furthermore, the cognitive revolution led to the acceptance of phenomena such as thoughts, although these were seen as programmed scripts that were accumulated across the life-time. Because the programs that supposedly underlay our thinking and experience simply became more sophisticated across development, such conceptions are also seen as quantitative – that is, children are not qualitatively different from adults.

A more recent wave of development arises from the neuropsychological revolution. The invention of increasingly advanced techniques for investigating brain processes (i.e. electroencephalography, transcranial magnetic stimulation, radiography, functional magnetic resonance imaging) allows a greater detail in understanding how neurophysiology and anatomy relate to psychological processes. Because the growth of the brain can be mapped from childhood to adulthood, a series of gradual changes can be observed, giving neuropsychological research a distinctly quantitative flavour.

Finally, at a societal level approaches are mixed as to how development is understood. On the one hand, laws prevent child labour, protect children from child abuse, premature sexual encounters, smoking, some forms of exploitation, and alcohol. Curricula to some extent reflect children's different needs: there is usually more art in the early years of school, and less studying for exams. On the other hand, children are often treated precisely as if they were mini-adults (House, 2000, 2006). Education is full of content that is too cognitively taxing or one-sided, puts young children under pressure to learn or experience the world in a one-sided way, or they are exposed to constant educational assessment (ibid.). The media consumption of children is often not concordant with their sensorimotor and physiological needs (see sections 5.3 and 8.5). The nutrition that many children receive is also inappropriate (section 6.6). Education and societal understanding of child development is still very 'quantitative', we maintain, but with the odd tribute paid to treating children as something other than mini-adults.

We largely find previous models of child development to be inadequate, paving the way for societal confusion and educational reforms that often place children's needs second. Essentially, a phenomenological-empirical and integrative view of child development has not made its way into mainstream thought in a sufficient way. Steiner's conception of child development is precisely this – a view that is both spiritual and physiological, phenomenological and experimental. Hence we outline Steiner's formulation next.

5.2 The anthroposophical view of human development across the lifespan

[O]ur basic concept or vision of the nervous system – as a sort of machine or computer – is radically inadequate, and needs to be supplemented by concepts more dynamic, more alive.

(Sacks, 2015, p. 91)

Steiner's view of child development was, as previously mentioned, both phenomenological and physiological, both quantitative and qualitative. He endeavoured to see how certain qualities or phases manifested both in terms of children's psychological-intellectual[10] as well as physiological-anatomical development. Steiner's approach was unique in that he applied careful methods of research in relation to the qualitative, physically invisible aspects, and hence his conception takes on a complexity and profundity that to many people initially seems overwhelming.

Again, Steiner's threefold view of the human being is paramount in understanding his view of child development. This threefold view (see section 3.3) emphasizes that three dimensions or spheres are responsible for human experience, namely the physical-bodily, the soul-psychological and the intellectual-spiritual. These three aspects of the human being tend to dominate at different points of human development, giving rise to the qualitative and quantitative differences that have been so keenly debated in the past, as mentioned at the beginning of this section. Next in this chapter, we outline the importance that Steiner placed on autonomy in human development (freehood), which serves as the guiding principle for an education in accordance with an understanding of development itself. For this reason, we then describe this development, from infancy to adulthood.

5.2.1 Developing freehood

For excessive freedom is nothing more than excessive slavery.

(Plato)

One unique feature of Steiner's ideas on child development and education is the immense importance he attaches to freedom. Technically, the meaning of the word freedom as intended by Steiner, and by the German language in which he spoke of it, is freehood, which is closer to the German *Freiheit*.[11] Freedom tends to refer to being free from external constraints to be able to do what one wishes. In contrast, the word 'freehood' refers more to learning to develop the capacity to act freely.[12] From a philosophical point of view, one is only free in doing what one wishes if that which one wishes is not subjected to external compulsion. For example, if I want to drink alcohol because I want to fit in with others, or because the thought of a drink dominates my spare moments, then I am not free, but subservient to social compulsion, on the one hand, and my psychophysiology on the other.

The distinction between freedom and freehood may at first sound trivial, but it is actually very important in education as it leads us to consider whether allowing children to have whatever they wish is helpful or hindering their development of freehood. Indeed, giving children what they wish may be considered freedom; however, if doing so leads to long-term character weakness, then their freehood is compromised by freedom. Accordingly, considering what freehood is and how it comes into being constitute a crucial riddle for child development.

Children who are simply images of their parents, unfreely following in their footsteps, may not be free in the true sense, nor are those who oppose everything their environment offers them likely to be free, but instead enslaved by contrariness or oppositionality. From a neuropsychological point of view, freehood is dependent on the ability to inhibit desires and weigh up choices. The term for this used in modern neuropsychology is 'executive functioning', which is associated with the part of the brain that is very small in animals, but large in comparison to human beings, and continues developing into the third decade of life (Fuster, 2002). From an anthroposophical point of view, one would call the executive functions 'I' functions, and Steiner also argued that the human 'I' does not really incorporate itself properly into the human organism until from around the third decade of life.

In the next section, we detail how, according to Steiner, this incorporation of the human 'I' occurs. One way of viewing development is by dividing it, among other possibilities, into phases lasting for approximately seven years, which is the division we adopt in this chapter. Given that the first seven years are most relevant for early childhood education, we focus mostly on these.

5.2.2 Early childhood (birth to dentition)

Children are born with a rich tapestry of experience gathered in utero and, according to Steiner, who believed in life before conception, they bring latent talents and abilities with them, which they seek to realise in their individual life's motif. In the mother's womb, children likely receive sensory input from the senses of touch, life, balance, movement, warmth, hearing and probably also speech (Bradley and Mistretta, 1975). At birth, babies have shown body awareness and perception (Filippetti et al., 2013).

Research has also analysed the limb movements of foetuses at 14, 18 and 22 weeks. Such analyses provide insight into sensory development because purposeful limb movements depend on the senses of movement and touch. At 14 weeks, foetuses could move limbs but were not yet able to direct these to targets in a coordinated manner (Zoia et al., 2007). However, clear evidence of purposeful motor control at age 22 weeks has been found, and to some extent even at 18 weeks. Finally, coupled with findings that new-born infants prefer the sound of their own mothers' and fathers' voices – and even the music accompanying television programmes frequently viewed by the mother during pregnancy – this suggests that speech perception also begins developing prenatally (Ruben, 1997). Undoubtedly, future work will uncover more aspects of development pre-birth.

We return now to the idea that, at birth, the qualitative (i.e. the soul-spiritual) is only a small way on in its journey to unite itself with the quantitative (i.e. physical) body of the child. From a phenomenological point of view, the new-born physical child has been formed predominantely out of the forces of the mother. If a child is to become an individuality as opposed to a mere copy of its parents and environment, it has to expend a good deal of time and effort teaching, forming and reshaping its body.

According to Steiner, the first and crucially important phase of child development runs from birth to the first dentition (i.e. the change of teeth). According to Steiner, development usually proceeds in approximately seven-year rhythms because the more permanent substances in the human body physically renew themselves approximately every seven years (Wade, 2005). To understand the significance of this, it is important to again reflect on the constant tangle of the qualitative and quantitative in Steiner's philosophy. A physical renewal enables a new quality to emerge, in the same way that when a tree changes leaves, a new quality (i.e. season) emerges. The hard bony substance formed early in this seven-year phase of development, that is the baby teeth, is replaced around the seventh year of life, thus indicating the transition to a new phase of development (Lievegoed, 2005). However, it is important not to fixate too strongly on the dentition, for this is only one of many physiological-anatomical indicators of this change in development (e.g. head to torso ratio, facial development).

Given the phenomenal changes occurring in the first seven years of human life, it is no surprise that in this first phase, Steiner afforded an important role to children's growth and physical development. This strong focus on the development of the body indicates that the will of the child is in particular developing in this phase of life, because this has an affinity to the limbs and metabolic system.

The will has several unique properties outlined earlier that have particular significance for education (see Chapter 6). First, the will is unconscious, and accordingly educational methods at this stage should also be less conscious (e.g. via imitation – see 6.1). Secondly, children's wills are malleable to environmental influences, which gives them an extraordinary capacity to imitate and absorb that to which they are exposed in their environment. Thirdly, the will forms the foundational capacity that will later allow the 'I' to carry out its unique impulses in life. If children are to develop freehood, then it is important that their wills are sown with qualities that later bear fruit.

This capacity to imitate, the necessity of grasping hold of the body, shaping it, and the amount of learning that occurs through experience mean that, according to Steiner, good educational methods in this first phase capitalize on: (a) learning by imitation and doing; (b) utilizing good role models in the environment; and (c) avoiding explanations that place too strong a demand on the intellect. For example, sitting down and reasoning with a four- or five year-old as to why he or she needs to tidy up, no matter how great the exhortation, is usually counter-productive (without some kind of explicit incentive – but which then brings other problems). It is far more effective to announce the tidying-up activity through some kind of routine, and for an adult to lead by example.

Additionally, Steiner also argued that the forces of growth are the same forces that later lay the foundation for thinking. For this reason, too much strain on the forces of thinking in this first phase can interfere with growth, and weaken the constitution. This idea may seem initially difficult to grasp for the modern mind that tends to see the brain as responsible for thinking, and its development dependent on stimulation and entirely separate from organ growth. Phenomenologically, however, one can observe the link between forces of growth and repair and thinking by observing how difficult it is to think when, for example, suffering from influenza. Anatomically, much brain growth in the first seven years is dependent on both environmental stimulation and innate growth. Thus, there is a role for both ensuring adequate stimulation and not interfering with the establishment of key neurological milestones (Perry, 2002); and as we later argue, this best takes the form of gentle sensory and language experiences largely through self-initiated play (see section 5.3 and Chapter 6).

Each seven-year phase can be divided approximately into a phase in which body, soul and spiritual development is particularly observable. From birth until around age of 2⅓ years, the physical development of the child is most marked. After birth the child is exposed to a raft of new sense impressions (visual, taste, warmth) that also vary in intensity in comparison to the sheltered life in the womb. Sounds are much louder, weight is felt as heavier without the support of the amniotic fluid, the world is colder; and because the source of nutrition changes from the umbilical cord to the oral digestive tract, hunger begins to be felt. To a newborn child, the world must present as a confusing, overwhelming and invasive phenomenon (see section 5.3). To draw an analogy, adults find the first day of work in a new job taxing because of the many new tasks, impressions and people: imagine how this must be for a child going from the womb into the world!

Throughout this first sub-phase of life, limb movements become more coordinated, birth reflexes die out (McPhillips and Sheehy, 2004), senses become more integrated, and the child begins to locomote. High points are crawling and then walking, the latter usually occurring around the first year of life. Steiner attached great importance to the upright orientation of the human gait, seeing this as an expression of 'I' development (see section 4.2.4). Indeed, research has found that children's attainment of walking relates to their later thinking (Murray et al., 2006), which, as stated earlier, represents 'I' functions from an anthroposophical viewpoint. Standing and walking places the human being, phenomenologically speaking, under the equal influence of the forces of Earth and the Heavens – thus symbolizing freehood (see section 4.2.4).

Once motor development has reached a certain maturity, the body can become an especially good tool for the soul. Around the third year of life, the child begins to feel more deeply that it is not simply an extension of the mother or the environment, but that he or she is an active agent. Children begin to say 'I' to themselves and to others. Will-battles and temper tantrums become more common. Language development accelerates, from about 50 words at 18 months to 10,000 by age 6 (Diesendruck, 2009).

Around the sixth year of life, another subtle change begins to occur in that children seem able to reflect more on their surroundings, and they are able to inhibit their behaviour and articulate their needs. A kindergarten teacher interviewed in Drummond and Jenkinson (n.d.) describes it thus:

> They're more conscious somehow, their awareness is beginning to extend outwards, there's a kind of richness in what they are able to achieve, where their skills are, where their interests are … it is almost like the Renaissance part of the kindergarten…. The middle part of the kindergarten is that very beautiful time when there is this huge blossoming in their interests, in their skills, in their capabilities, what they can do, what they want to show that they can do … they can now take ideas and really run with them and create something quite amazing. *(p. 41)*

Nightmares may increase, and anxieties about losing a parent (e.g. through death, divorce or natural disaster) can be particularly unsettling. This broader perspective bears the character of the spirit making itself particularly present. Once the 'I' or spirit begins to manifest itself more strongly and feels itself as an individual, then it can begin to sense its separation and fallibility, which can lead to little crises and angsts.

5.2.3 Into middle childhood and adulthood

As previously discussed, the first phase of childhood is dominated by the development of the body, and the second phase is too, albeit with some important differences. Clearly, important growth marks the transition to puberty in comparison to the rest of the body. Baby fat is lost, bodies become longer and thinner and the head less over-sized (Lievegoed, 2005). Faces lose some of the universal baby look and come to more closely resemble the child as he or she will look in adulthood. Sensory processes and motor development are still immature (see section 5.3).

In this phase of life, just as imitation is the key to education in the first seven years, according to Steiner the relationship to the educator is crucial.[13] Because the child is becoming more and more conscious of both the outside world and inner changes, a stable, authentic and reliable relationship to educators and parents is important. Expressed from a different point of view, whereas imitation and education through the will were important in the first phase of development, in this second phase children can be educated through the feeling. Stories filled with morally inspiring characters as well as stable personal relationships can be used to instil freehood in children. Given this focus on the development of emotion (and the inevitable associated emotionality of this phase of development), as well as the still appreciable growth that is occurring, for Steiner it is still too early to really tax children intellectually. Instead, providing children with aesthetically and rhythmically appealing content is an effective educational means (e.g. learning rhymes, hearing stories, singing, music, drawing, physical movement and so on).

Just as the child approaching the third year of life typically undergoes a phase of strongly feeling itself as an individuality, a similar experience occurs one third of the way into this second phase. The child inwardly crosses 'the Rubicon'[14] from which there is no going back…. This can be experienced as a mini-adolescence, with children realising that they are individuals, that their parents have flaws and that they have to go out into the world. Often parents report that their child has simply become unreasonable, like an adolescent. However, this is an important step in developing self-awareness, and should not be discouraged or admonished, but instead ideally met with understanding and humour.

Puberty is the external sign for another change, most notable for the emergence of a strong and often initially chaotic soul life. Children struggle to grasp hold of this swarm of feelings and increased self-awareness, resulting in the often-tumultuous adolescent years. However, again Steiner is consistent with Jean Piaget in seeing that the intellect undergoes a new birth, and can begin to develop more strongly. Across the life-span, the first 21 years are primarily concerned with the body, the next 21 years with the soul, and from age 42 onwards more strongly with 'I' or spiritual development. However, within each of these phases, further finer gradations can be observed (Lievegoed, 1985).

5.3 Sensory development

Steiner once remarked that the human being at birth is almost entirely sense organ (Grunelius, 1950/1991). Before turning to see how this manifests physically, it is interesting to consider the role of the senses in child development. As outlined earlier in Chapter 4, the human being has numerous senses that provide direct links between the environment and the child's experience. In other words, the senses are the mediators between the outer world and the child's inner world. To say that children are nearly 'entirely sense organ' at birth is another way of saying that they have not yet developed independent inner worlds of ideas, memories and experiences, such that they live more strongly in the numerous sense impressions approaching them from the outside world. In other words, the child is at one with the world, for better or worse, and needs to draw itself back from the world to develop individuality. The development of the senses allows the child to do this, to perceive the world, instead of directly living with the world.

Viewed physically, the head of the new born is large, and the limbs and torso small in comparison (Lievegoed, 2005). Besides a few primitive survival reflexes that usually die out some time after birth (Berk, 2004), the human new born is entirely unable to fend for itself. Also, in comparison to animals, the human brain is comparatively underdeveloped at birth, experiencing much postnatal development (Perry, 2002). Interestingly, this comparatively immature development at birth allows for greater human freedom because less development is determined by biology than is possible in other mammals and animals.

In this chapter we outline the development of the senses in the child, with a focus on features and principles affecting them. Crucially, we as adults have forgotten what an incredible and taxing struggle it was to learn to perceive and thrive in the world of the senses. This forgetting leads to many educational errors in early childhood that likely impede children in their development. We now outline eight such principles.

5.3.1 The world outside forms the sense organ inside

We tend to think that our sense organs are 'just there', that their development is innate and self-evident. Nothing could be further from the truth. As previously mentioned in this book, Steiner was heavily influenced by Goethe and his phenomenological understanding of the senses. In contrast to more simplistic conceptions around at the time, Goethe believed that the eye was formed by light. In other words, using a given sense stimulates the development of that organ. We now know, from rather cruel experiments on animals and in the case of child neglect, that depriving children of sensory experiences during the early formative years can permanently damage or prevent senses from developing (Perry, 2002; Steiner, 1999). Hence the first principle of sensory development – that sensory qualities and experience shape and school the senses. It also follows that a rich, varied sensory environment should help a child's sensory organs develop optimally (see section 6.4).

5.3.2 All in good time…

Sense organs require time to develop, to calibrate to the surroundings, to integrate with other senses, so as to become subtle organs of perception.

Physically, sensory development entails development of organs and receptors, the formation of neural synapses and their connection to the receptors and finally, via sensory stimulation, the brain itself undergoes changes (Neuffer, 2008). In fact, this process happens remarkably early in life, by around the second month of pregnancy (Schepers and Ringkamp, 2009). The hearing and vestibular organs begin forming very early in foetal development (at least by the time the foetus is 3mm in length), and have reached the development that they have at birth by about five months pre-partum. Taste buds have been identified on the foetal tongue at around 8–9 weeks (Fulkerson, 2014). Similarly, touch receptors begin their development early, and by about seven weeks gestation, the foetus shows reflexive response to stimulation (Neuffer, 2008). The visual organs begin developing early and undergo their major developmental milestones between the second and fifth months, before continuing development after birth (ibid.).

Anatomical development is only one aspect. A second is trying to understand when we begin to experience impressions from the senses. Hearing responses have been established from around 19 weeks of pregnancy (Vriens et al., 2014). Tactile memory for objects has been established in 28-week-old pre-term babies (Steiner, 1925/1997).

In short, there is mounting evidence that the foetus develops its sensory organs in the subtle pre-birth environment. Despite the womb being largely sealed off from light and sound, foetuses show response to sound and light. There are also in utero variations in warmth, movement, body orientation and salinity of amniotic fluid which, combined, provide a subtle but rich pre-birth environment. After birth, whole new intensities and ranges of sensory experience are possible. Coming to grips with this all requires good time.

5.3.3 Everything at its right time

For the development of sensory organs, timing is key. By timing, we mean that there are certain periods – or 'windows' – in development in which children need to develop certain sensory abilities, or it will be too difficult later, or possibly too late altogether (Perry, 2002). In these periods, the central nervous system appears particularly plastic, meaning that the brain is malleable to sensory influences from the outside (Trachtenberg, 2015). Such sensitive periods have been found for the auditory, visual and sensorimotor systems in humans and animals (Berardi et al., 2000). In terms of Steiner's speech sense, there also seems to be a similar window for healthy development. Children who have hearing difficulties early in life and only later have these corrected suffer lasting speech perception difficulties (Polka et al., 2009; Ruben, 1997).

Children need appropriate sensory experiences, from pre-birth onwards, and ideally without phases of deprivation.

5.3.4 Too much can be too little

> The baby, assailed by eyes, ears, nose, skin, and entrails at once, feels it all as one great blooming, buzzing confusion.
>
> *(William James)*

A common idea in early childhood education is that children need stimulation for their development. This desire to stimulate, capture and maintain attention results in ever-more brazen marketing techniques, and in the world of children a new breed of toys – toys that flash bright lights, blurt out various supposedly 'educational' noises and programmes that 'educate' children. Moreover, modern society seems to be both fast-paced and specialized, creating a compulsion to seek out experiences that round out the sometimes one-sided experience that goes hand in hand with this specialization. Perhaps the ghost that whispers in parents' and teachers' ears, calling for ever-more stimulation, in part comes from studies showing how healthy development is simply not possible without social interaction and input (Perry, 2002).

However, sensory overstimulation, or one-sided stimulation in the form of, for example, lights and sound, but neglecting the social senses, is misguided for two reasons. First, in sensory development there is a principle called 'the concept of limitations' (Lewkowicz, 2000). This states that if one sense is not being strongly stimulated, then another can develop without competition. In other words, a child has less opportunity to focus on developing touch and movement senses if obtrusive visual and auditory input is constantly present, as happens during fast-paced electronic media. Secondly, the role of subtlety is important. More and more stimulation could be expected to develop perception of loud and intense noises, whereas subtle exposure could be reasonably expected to lead to the development of fine sensory differentiation. Because the pre-birth environment provides subtle sensory stimulation, perhaps post-birth stimulation – at least initially – should also be gentle and subtle in order to provide continuity and transition into middle childhood (Neuffer, 2008).

5.3.5 Senses work together

> [W]e see things in the following way: in presenting an arrangement of colours to us, they show also the boundaries of these colours – lines and forms. But we do not usually attend to the way we actually

perceive. If a man perceives a coloured circle he simply says: I see the colour, I see also the curve of the circle, the form of the circle. But there we have two completely different things looked upon as one. What you immediately perceive through the real activity of the eye, apart from the other senses, is only the colour. You see the form of the circle by making use of the sense of movement in your sub-consciousness…

(Steiner, 1919/1993, p. 148)

As the above quotation makes clear, Steiner thought that the act of seeing a circle, for example, required the working together of the vision and movement senses. This process of two senses working together is called 'sensory integration'. In real-world environments, it is rare that only one sense at a time is stimulated; usually, several are stimulated at once. When hearing a loud thump, for example, we may also feel a vibration (sense of movement) and the floor shaking (sense of balance, sense of movement). Despite this multisensory stimulation, we experience phenomena as unified entities.[15] Exactly how we do this is unknown! At any rate, the ability to transfer and integrate information from one sense to another, and more than one sense at a time, develops early in life; it has even been observed in new-born infants (Slater et al., 1997).

Generally, sensory integration refers to the senses working together to provide a better percept[16] than one sense alone can provide (Brandwein et al., 2011). Crucially for early years education, the ability to integrate information across senses requires much time to develop, not reaching adult levels until at least puberty (Ernst, 2008; Gori et al., 2008; Rentschler, 2004). This suggests that early education needs to provide children with rich and authentic sensory stimulation across multiple senses.

5.3.6 Perceiving is more than sensing

Because sensory development is automatic in adults, we tend to overlook what an impressive achievement something as simple as recognizing a table in a room is! Recent research suggests that acquiring knowledge through the senses is an intricate interplay between thinking processes and sensory input (Trachtenberg, 2015). Interestingly, in his seminal work *The Philosophy of Freedom*, this is precisely what Steiner proposed; an 'I' directing conceptual activity unites with bottom-up sensory stimulation to result in the act of knowing (Steiner, 1918/1986). To make this process comprehensible and show just what is required for a child to master something as simple as 'seeing' a table, consider the steps involved:

1. Children need to first develop the organs of vision, touch, movement and balance. Balance helps children recognize the orientation of the table, movement its depth, touch the difference between texture and distance (e.g. is an object darker because it is rougher, or because it's further away?).
2. They need to have used these senses and to have physically explored objects in the past so that they can make sense of visual cues (such as depth, perspective, that overlayed objects are in front).
3. Children have to be able to move to the object to carry out the investigations necessary for 1 and 2. For this they need motor skills.
4. They also need to have a concept for 'table'. Likely, a child will have to have experienced many different tables to be able to realise that a table is generally a flat surface, supported by a legged structure, about the height of a human lap – either adult or child size – when a person is sitting on a chair or stool. Before this can be realised, a child has to understand surface, legs, human adult, human child, sitting, stool, chair etc. So they may need many other concepts first before they can recognize the concept of a table itself.
5. Finally, a child needs to view the scene and recognize the table, after having gone through steps 1 through 4 many times with other tables. How quickly and easily a child will recognize the object in the room as a table will depend on the richness of perceptual experience and thinking.

In short, seeing and recognizing requires a rich tapestry of past experience that requires time and cultivation to develop.

5.3.7 The shift from seeing qualities to seeing ideas becomes habit

Generally speaking, we move from seeing qualities to seeing ideas. As adults, we look at the world, and seldom stop to admire the qualities in the world. Our perceptual system is constantly perceiving, identifying and judging as we hurry through the world. Children, on the other hand, seem to delight more in the qualities, stopping to investigate and gather new impressions, sometimes asking 'What is that?'. Many artists try to recapture this primeval aesthetic state, this naivety, to see the world through children's eyes. How is it that we lose this unbiased unison with the world?

From an anthroposophical point of view, the recognition of novel objects requires joining perceptual with conceptual activity (section 5.3.6). Much of what we believe that we perceive is actually idea. Thus, there are no straight lines, objects or the like that exist purely perceptually to the senses. For the sense of sight, all there is are gradations of colour; and for the sense of sound, gradations of tone. What we perceive in the environment in the form of lines and objects is the idea or phenomenon of the object revealing itself to us through the senses and through concepts (see section 4.4.3). To the senses, there is no reason to consider a picture on the wall as being separate from the wall itself. The picture is a phenomenon created by the artist and recognized by us as a piece of artwork because we have learned to perceive the idea of art presented in that form. Thus, for children the surrounding world is more of a riddle to them, which enables them to interact with it and delight in it in ways that we often can no longer do.

5.3.8 Disturbed senses, disturbed development

As previously outlined, the journey to becoming a fully perceiving adult is a long and even perilous journey. It is interesting that there are a number of developmental disorders where disturbed sensory development, and in particular sensory integration, is a hallmark feature. For instance, children with autism spectrum disorder (Goulardins et al., 2013; Sanz-Cervera et al., 2017) often show sensory delay and even a hypersensitivity to some forms of experience, such as human touch or preferring strong earthy smells. Some children with a condition known as developmental coordination disorder (Michel et al., 2011) have trouble mastering their bodies and developing coordinated movement. Still others with learning disabilities often show sensory anomalies (Pieters et al., 2012; Westendorp et al., 2011).

Moreover, children have at birth around 70 birth reflexes, which are automated movements in response to stimuli (e.g. grasping, swimming, turning head). Normally, these reflexes become inhibited – that is, they fade away because they are no longer needed for survival. However, research has discovered that when these reflexes persist, behavioural and learning problems can result (Konicarova and Bob, 2012; McPhillips and Sheehy, 2004; see also Goddard Blythe, 2011, 2018).

The question of why senses relate to learning and developmental delays is unclear. However, by considering exactly what sensory development involves, we may come a step closer to understanding. As previously mentioned, perceiving, recognizing and knowing are complex human achievements that require the whole body, functioning senses, and the coming together of the human spirit with its soul and body. The existence of disorders relating to both sensory and learning problems serves as a warning to educators to take the senses seriously in the early years, and beyond.

In a Nutshell

- Views of child development are numerous, giving rise to a diverse range of theories, from psychodynamic, behavioural, neuropsychological, to cognitive views.

- Steiner viewed child development from a unique and comprehensive perspective, emanating from his phenomenological research.

- Educating children to freehood is a key goal – freehood entailing the capacity to act in accordance with one's true self, being less governed by feeling or bodily constraints.

- Children's development from pre-birth to the first change of teeth and beyond follows both quantitative and qualitative phases, each helping the child to unfold into an adult capable of freehood.

- Children's senses also develop across childhood, in particular from pre-natal to middle childhood.

- Principles of sensory development govern what educational experiences are harmful and helpful for the developing child.

.

CHAPTER 6

The Educational Principles:
Educating to Freehood

As we have attempted to outline in the first chapters of this book, Steiner education is built on numerous considerations about how the child develops. These lead to specific educational principles that can be formulated in a number of different ways. However, if there were to be one key principle that hovers above all the rest, it would be that the purpose of Steiner education is to facilitate the development of freehood (see section 5.2.1).

Returning to the idea of freehood, Steiner is ahead of his time in that he recognized that the freedom of the individual would increasingly take centre stage in society. This view was formed at a time when three competing ideas for shaping human development dominated. On the one hand, genetics- and biology-based principles of human development arising from the newly discovered Darwinism were popular. Such ideas lead, according to Steiner, to an overly strong focus on the biology, thus imprisoning humankind into racial confines. The second idea competing for societal development was that of ethnicity and/or nationality. Although recognizing the reality that one's socialization, language and culture play an important role in shaping personality, Steiner saw the danger that focusing on groups of people would lead to endless division and suffering.[17] Moreover, Steiner was against one-sided conceptions of freedom, whereby self-gratification is mistaken for freedom.

Briefly, Steiner considered developing human freedom as being the central task of human evolution (Steiner, 1997). As outlined earlier, we adopted the coinage 'freehood' in order to differentiate what Steiner intended by freedom from the latter's common usage. For Steiner, freehood entailed being able to act out of the higher part of oneself, out of the human 'I', in accordance with its own nature – according to one's true self. Much of what we ascribe to our personality, such as profession, preference, culture or family traits, is only distally related to our true self, so acting out of needs arising from these levels is seldom truly free. Hence, as educators we have an immense task to understand freedom, freehood and how children can actually experience freedom on their way to freehood. Freedom might be given, but freehood can only be developed by an individual person.

Developing freehood is an eminently educational task, and an extremely difficult one at that. In the first seven years of life, this requires three aspects. First, children needed to be educated in a way that is in accordance with their growing individuality. Nicol and Taplin call this protecting the forces of childhood (2012). Such protection of childhood includes recognizing children's natural impulse to imitate (section 6.1), explore (6.2), to live in imagination (6.3), and to develop their senses so that they can properly perceive the world (5.3) and aesthetically nourish the child (6.4). Secondly, they need to be free to feel the consequences of their own actions, but at the same time be protected via rhythm, structure and security (section 6.5), under the wise and watchful guidance of the educators (6.7). Thirdly, children need to be protected from the intrusions of the outside world where possible, which includes nutrition (section 6.6) and developmentally appropriate educational opportunities (8.3, 8.5). Of course, as children progress beyond the early years, the relative importance of each of these principles changes, and freehood can increasingly be realised if a healthy development has been achieved in other domains.

6.1 Imitation: The teacher as a role model

> Steiner teachers often refer to the importance and power of 'imitation' in children's lives, but this is not to suggest any falseness or insincerity on the part of the child who imitates her teacher. The everyday use of the word to suggest an inferior substitute for the real thing (imitation cream, fur or pearls) has no application here. The children copy their teachers as clerks once copied precious manuscripts; their copying asserts and extends the value of the original.
>
> *(Drummond, 2011, p. 95)*

Role modelling and imitation are described by Steiner as the leitmotif most encapsulating early childhood education. Both principles, being intrinsically related, are foundational in forming and guiding children's development and interactions with their environments. In this section, we first outline imitation, before turning to the teacher's role-model function.

6.1.1 Imitation

For Rudolf Steiner, the natural capacity to imitate was the innate force upon which early childhood education should focus and capitalize (Steiner, 1924/2004). Such a philosophy was in stark contrast to Steiner's contemporaries – for example, Sigmund Freud or the behaviourists – who focused on pleasure and reinforcement as the determining factors in human behaviour and learning. Interestingly, in recent times social and neuroscientific research has begun to point towards the important role of imitation in multiple areas of child development, particularly the three major achievements of early childhood – walking, speaking and thinking – as well as the recognition of imitation of adults' expressions and empathy (Carr et al., 2003; Heyes, 2001).

The intrinsic interest that children unconsciously possess is clearly observed when, for example, taking a walk with a young child, who pauses every two steps to closely watch another child, an animal or a builder working on a house. In the sense that that which a child observes is readily imitated in the child's own play or interactions, it can be said that children possess a certain oneness or harmony with the world. This connection to the world makes experience for children an intensely sense-based one (section 5.3) which is then reflected in children's inner, imaginative life (6.4). Steiner termed this connection a 'religiosity', which would today perhaps be expressed as an embodied devotion to the surrounding environment. Although this description may sound curious at first pass, the linguistic roots of the word religious are 'religio', meaning 'bond' or 'reverence'; and going further back 're', meaning 'again', and 'bind/connect', thus to re-connect. Essentially, then, Steiner is referring to the special awe in which children observe the world.

By looking at children's development, many examples of imitation are observable. For example, the first babbling of an infant across the first months begins to more closely resemble the native language to which that child is exposed. Gradually, first the melody and then the vowels, consonants and words emerge (Polka et al., 2009).

Observing a child beginning to walk is also a fascinating experience. For all intents and purposes, infants have a comfortable life, lying on the floor, being attended to and having their needs met. For some reason, they throw comfort to the wind and begin to roll over, sit up, position themselves on all fours, crawl, pull themselves up against objects; and despite the many falls and accidents, they learn to walk. As discussed by Humbert de Superville and Steiner, the upright position is important for human development (section 4.2.4), distinguishing us from animals. Case studies suggest that children (so-called feral children) who were raised by animals and not exposed to human walking do not learn to walk and act like humans, but instead are like the animals that raised them (McNeil et al., 1984). Just as with language, children do not need to be taught to walk, such as with walkers – in fact, doing so appears to be harmful or useless (Pin et al., 2007); rather, walking arises naturally through their desire to imitate and an inner impulse to stand vertically. This experience of walking is so strong and formative that feral children often also experience physical changes from not doing so (e.g. deformation of the toes, hair growth, jumping abilities, spinal changes – McNeil et al., 1984).

By the second year of life, but particularly from the fifth year of life, most young children demonstrate broader behaviours that are recognizable as imitation (Heyes, 2001). Such acts become quite sophisticated – for example, when a child cuts fruit, sweeps the floor, uses a branch to 'mow' the lawn, bakes a cake in the sandpit, or independently collects his or her shoes when it is time to go out. For this reason, the child's ability to imitate is viewed as the most important method of learning, as across the course of time, this capacity helps to lay down important skills on the path to independence. The art of teaching this age of child is to capitalize on this capacity for imitation, and provide young children with worthy role models. In contrast, adults who learn a second language can soon lament the loss of this imitative drive, finding that new words and sounds do not come so easily as they do for children.

6.1.2 Being a role model

Essentially, every adult in a child's environment is a potential role model, as children will imitate familiar or favoured adults very readily. Most parents learn this lesson quite poignantly when they start seeing their own mannerisms or (colourful!) language reflected back at them. In this sense, being a role model for a child is not a matter of choice, nor a matter of arrogance or superiority, but simply the reality of a child's natural urge to imitate. In the same way, asking children not to copy something dangerous that an adult is doing is seldom effective, as children have such a strong automatic urge to imitate such that they can hardly help themselves. From the educational perspective of the teacher, this process of imitation is often also an opportunity or prompt for self-reflection (see section 6.10).

With the awareness of their position as a role model in mind, teachers in Waldorf-Steiner kindergartens endeavour to carry out many of the daily activities around kindergarten in conjunction with the children. Household and artistic activities such as cooking, baking, sewing, carving or singing can all be an impetus for children's own imaginative play. This type of imitation in play is a developmentally appropriate, ideal way for children to extend their own capabilities and repertoire of skills.

Given the importance in early childhood placed upon learning through experience and via imitation, Steiner considered it important to keep intellectual stimulation to a minimum – for example, by avoiding diffuse, abstract explanations for the nature of phenomena. From an anthroposophical perspective (see section 6.9), overstimulation of the intellect at an early age depletes the forces available for a child's body, brain and sensory development (McKeen, 2011). As such, the focus in Waldorf education is on developing the necessary abilities for later intellectual development through doing, which in turn schools the will. Parents and teachers may notice that an intellectual explanation for why a process occurs (e.g. why we wash our hands before preparing food) may be lost on a child, but its demonstration can have a lasting effect.

With this in mind, it follows that particularly child-appropriate interactions are those in which requests are accompanied by a pictorial, graspable and tangible image. For example, rather than saying 'Sit up straight', a teacher might say 'Sit like a king'. The image of a towering king is more powerful and takes precedence over the verbal request, as it is more concrete and tangible for children. As such, the saying 'Do as I say, not as I do' is precisely at odds with the Waldorf-Steiner approach, and runs counter to a child's desire to do 'as I do'.

6.2 Imagination and free play

> The urge to play between the ages of two and a half and five is really
> just the externalized activity of a child's power of fantasy.
> *(Steiner, 1921–1922/2003, p. 113)*

One of the unique features of early years Steiner education is its recognition of the first phase of childhood as being inherently phenomenological. Children in this phase naturally seek out and experience the world in its entirety. Thereby, full sensory experiences of the surrounding world, alongside inner experiences of the developing 'I' as it finds its way gradually into its increasing capacity to consciously think, are important. The element in which children live in the early years is therefore both thoroughly bodily-dependent through the senses and desire to master the body, and imaginative through children's rich inner life. In this section we focus on how, in Steiner education, the imagination of the child is developed.

6.2.1 Imagination

Another focus in Waldorf-Steiner kindergartens is to foster imagination and creative play (Waite and Rees, 2011). The capacity to imagine and be creative is indicative of the ability to create and live in a world of internal images, which is part of the process of developing an independent inner life (Taylor, 2013). This allows us to develop the special quality of being able to think and speak without the presence of any objects in the immediate environment (Piaget, 2003). The capacity to create mental images independent of the physical presence of an object contributes to intellectual abilities (Kosslyn et al., 1990), which often require exact conscious mental representations (Trionfi and Reese, 2009).

In most cases, imaginative development is not something that needs to be developed from outside sources, but instead is an innate childhood faculty that can only really be destroyed or neglected from outside, as cases of prolonged childhood neglect indicate. Most infants and small children will find ways to interact with their surroundings in novel and self-directed ways, as typified by the experience whereby young children often spend more time playing with the box in which a gift came rather than with the gift itself. The role of the educator is to provide this imagination with an appropriate content, thus paying careful attention to the kind of play materials available (section 6.3.2) and the aesthetic surroundings (section 6.4). Quite naturally, children's imaginative life will then incorporate that which has been offered, through a mixture of imitation and independent inner activity.

Although the ability to imagine appears to be fairly innate, it needs to be actively practised and cannot be neglected, or the capacity diminishes. Two influences can reduce self-initiated imaginative activity. Electronic-media exposure takes over much of the imagery generation (Valkenburg and van der Voort, 1994), as can adult interference during play (sometimes termed 'directed' or 'structured'

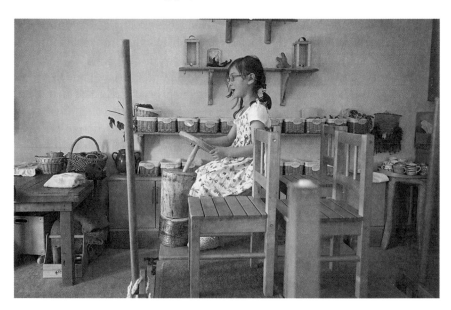

play), in which 'learning activities' or unwarranted interruption disrupts the flow of play. Examples of the latter include redirecting children's games, and interrupting them to ask them what they are playing. Even observing them while they are engaged in an imaginative game is often enough to make children aware of their earthly selves, tear them out of their imaginative worlds, and hence kill off the activity. Imaginative play is often a private affair, despite being acted out in front of adults, and should not be unnecessarily interrupted. Therefore, the focus in Steiner education is on providing play materials and activities that gently stimulate the imagination alongside the provision of much unstructured free play time, to which we turn next.

6.2.2 Free play

> Imagination in children represents the very forces that have just liberated themselves from performing similar creative work within the physical formation of the brain. This is why we must avoid, as much as possible, forcing these powers of imagination into rigid, finished forms.
>
> *(Steiner, 1921–1922/2003, p. 128)*

The true fruits of a child's self-initiated activity can be seen during free play. In the words of Friedrich Schiller in his letter on the aesthetic education of man, 'man only plays when he is truly human, and he is only truly human when he plays' (Schiller, 1795/2009, p. 93). In other words, far from amounting to trivial time-wasting and self-amusement, play is an integral part of the fabric of human existence! One reason for this is that play is an activity we engage in for the purpose of play itself – it is not a means to any other end and, as such, is one of the few areas of life in which we are truly free from outer compulsion.

One of the first Waldorf educators, Herbert Hahn, published a book called *On the Seriousness of Play* (1930/1988), in which he discussed in detail the importance of children's play. Playing is not simply 'messing around', a distraction from the more important tasks in life, as adults may sometimes believe. Rather, free play in which children can follow their own impulses and create a world around them as they see fit, without any particular purpose, is extremely important for their development. Steiner even went so far as to call play 'the work of children', pointing out that when children are playing, they are, in their own mind at least, working (Steiner, 1923/1996). Indeed, children can get into quite a huff when their play is interrupted!

In its essence, play is a natural, child-like way of discovering the world and oneself. A child can play at his or her own speed, appropriate to his or her individual level of development, and digest the experiences that he or she has, in peace. Play is a state in which anything that is not the focus of play retreats into insignificance.

Free play, which in contrast to guided play (Weisberg et al., 2016) is a form that is not directed from outside or by educators, allows a child to learn in a self-directed way, thereby laying the foundations for later development. The significance of play is also gaining recognition in the fields of education and developmental psychology (Golinkoff et al., 2006). Play has been credited with helping to develop motor, language, cognitive, social and imaginative capabilities (Ely and McCabe, 1994; Hall et al., 2013; Levine et al., 2012; Wallace and Russ, 2015).

From the perspective of Steiner education, play is also viewed as an activity through which important physical, intellectual and emotional (body, soul, spirit) development can occur, as play allows a forum for children's internal creative impulses to unfold. Providing sufficient outlets for play and movement to support a child's physical development – particularly in the modern technological, fast-paced world of today – takes on ever-greater significance. As such, Steiner education places particular emphasis on children having access to sufficient space, not only in the sense of time, and room in their environment, but also in terms of unrestrictive materials that allow a child's individuality and creativity to unfold through play (Nicol and Taplin, 2012).

6.3 Aesthetic experiences: music, nature and the arts

Waldorf-Steiner kindergartens are also characterized by the rich aesthetic surroundings and experiences available, which manifest in music, art, nature and language. For this reason it is perhaps not surprising that studies find that Steiner kindergarten children's drawings were rated as being more creative and having more artistic merit than those from not only state kindergartens, but also from Montessori early years institutions (Rose et al., 2012).

6.3.1 Artistic activities

> Complementary to any purely medicinal, or medical, approach
> there must also be an 'existential' approach: in particular, a sensitive
> understanding of action, art and play as being in essence healthy and
> free, and thus antagonistic to crude drives and impulsion.
> *(Sacks, 2015, p. 102)*

During free play, children often organize their surroundings in a creative, artistic way, for example by arranging objects into almost-geometric patterns or building huts out of play-silks, boxes and wooden clothes-frames. To allow this aesthetic potential to unfold, Waldorf-Steiner kindergartens focus on offering a variety of artistic activities, such as crayon drawing, water-colour painting, beeswax moulding, as well as other seasonal arts and crafts activities. Additionally, the natural world – such as in the garden or the forest – also provides a rich source of inspiration. Such activities can be a form of self-expression and a way to make a mark on the child's environment, be it in the form of soap bubbles on the mirror, a sandpit cake, or more obviously in a drawing. Both forms of artistic endeavour, those arising out of everyday play and those that are more directed, are valued in Steiner education. A range of tools and materials is often provided, such as wax crayons, beeswax, wool and wood, to allow children the opportunity to explore various artistic methods. Preparations for the various festivals also provide another artistic outlet (see section 6.4).

Music is also a constant companion in Steiner kindergartens. Song is used during festival celebrations and in the various activities. For example, bread preparation may be accompanied with a baker song, and circle-time also usually contains several songs. Song, along with finger-games, rhymes and verse, can also be an important tool in the educator's bag, to calm children when chaos is developing, initiate tidying up, or redirect children's attention. It is also important that the music is not provided via a loud-speaker, but is directly performed. This has numerous advantages, ranging from acoustics to authenticity, and early exposure to music is key to improving later pitch

perception. Children often quite naturally introduce songs from kindergarten into the home, such that parents often remark on the improvement in their child's singing after beginning early years Steiner education.

6.3.2 Sense-rich play materials

Particular consideration is also given to the choice of play materials in Waldorf-Steiner kindergartens. Generally, materials are made from those found in nature, such as wood, wool, silk and cotton. One important reason is that emphasis is placed on children experiencing nature in its primary form. This is particularly important in our synthetic, industrialized age, and helps children phenomenologically to learn the elementary properties tangled up in the diverse manifestations of the sense world (see Chapter 4). Items are typically simple, often without a pre-determined function or form, with the intention being to provide a greater breadth of opportunity for a child's own creative play.

Additionally, the simple, natural materials allow children to have differentiated, fine-grained, primary sense experiences, without being overwhelmed by, for example, flashing lights and loud sounds. Play items have generally undergone little to no processing and refinement, and remain as true to their original form and function as possible. For example, wooden blocks may consist of actual branches from trees, simply cut down into smaller pieces and oiled. Other commonly found 'unprocessed' play items include pine cones, shells, stones, bark or chestnuts. Cotton or silk cloths of various sizes are also popular, as well as crocheted woollen bands, or felted wool ropes.

Even the toys and play equipment that are more 'refined' and not borrowed directly from nature – for example, dolls – are kept deliberately simple. Waldorf dolls are typically made of cotton fabric stuffed with wool, with simple, undifferentiated limbs. Perhaps most notable, however, are their simple faces, where the eyes, nose and month are represented with a hint of coloured thread – quite in contrast to the sometimes overbearing smiling or laughing faces of most dolls commonly available (Grunelius, 1950/1991). As mentioned above, the intention here is to allow children greater freedom in their play; to allow them to decide which emotion their doll is currently experiencing, or whether it is awake or asleep.

Aside from allowing greater space for children's fantasy to shape their play, the natural, 'imperfect' play objects in a Waldorf-Steiner kindergarten also allow more opportunities to develop basic skills, such as learning about balance and estimation. For example, building a tower with a selection of unplaned wooden branches is distinctly more challenging than placing many uniform, square blocks on top of one another! In this way, children also come to appreciate the diverse qualities of the natural world without the expectation that all objects will neatly stack into, or on top of, one another. These types of experiences with the world also naturally foster problem solving and lateral thinking abilities. Furthermore, the use of natural materials that have not

been treated removes the concern of children being exposed to chemicals that may not be safe.

Lastly, another category of play objects comprises of items not typically thought of as toys – for example, watering cans, dust pans and brushes, or cooking utensils. However, given children's imitative and imaginative abilities, such objects readily become toys in kindergarten life.

6.3.3 Language

The ability to use language is a uniquely human activity that not only allows communication, but imbues and suffuses our surroundings with culture, soul, melody and aesthetic mood. Conversely, language that is dry, abstract and relentless works in a parching way on the environment. For this reason, the type of language and when it is employed constitute a cornerstone of Steiner education.

Depending on the culture but especially in English, language today has a tendency to become abstract, which makes it difficult for children to relate to. One property of abstract language is the inundation of technical terms that have lost their connection to the morphemes comprising the word. This is particularly evident in the English academic penchant for Latin words, or in the increasing introduction of English words into many languages, which replaces original words that have naturally evolved from constituent parts (i.e. morphemes) in those languages.

Another feature of abstract language is the tendency to name everything (e.g. 'Look, that is called an "aviary"'), as opposed to more characterizing evocations (e.g. 'Imagine living in that bird house!'). A characteristic or adjective, when well chosen, evokes a feeling, and alludes to the nature of things, whereas a substantive (i.e. a noun) often does not invoke the same curiosity. Of course adjectives can also be judgmental and basal, such as overuse of words like 'ugly' or 'silly'. Interestingly, it is often dialects that capture this more living, soul quality, such as when in Cockney a hammer is referred to as a 'jimmy jammer'.

In addition, a living language need not be artificially simplified for children and conveyed in a patronizing tone, as if the child is half-deaf and intellectually sub-par. It is far better to speak in an authentic way ('I' sense; see section 4.4.4 and also section 6.6.1), leaving children to utilize their speech and thought senses to extract the meaning and its essence, and their extraordinary imitation abilities to absorb the word.

Through verses, rhymes, finger games, songs and stories, in Waldorf-Steiner kindergartens a particular emphasis is placed on language and music. Be it during circle-time or story-time, or simply during transition phases, attention is given to the rhythmic, poetic elements of language. Basic word-games may also be employed. Indeed, a full and pictorial use of language in a nuanced and conscious fashion can provide teachers with opportunities to enlighten, to comfort, to use humour and to allude to the wonders of the surrounding world. In particular, when combined with music and rituals, a thoughtful use of language has the ability to create an especially calming, aesthetically rich environment.

Most Steiner kindergartens also perform puppet shows, as well as finger games and songs accompanied by gestures. The focus on the aesthetic and rhythmic nature of language allows even non-native speakers to gradually acquire the new language, particularly in terms of the rhythmical (phonetic and prosodic) and semantic (meaning) aspects of the language, but also its structure (grammar) and pragmatics (contextual meaning).

Story-telling, sometimes in the form of a free rendering, is also important in Waldorf-Steiner kindergartens. And although both a story-reading and a free rendering can improve language acquisition (Suggate, Lenhard, Neudecker and Schneider, 2013), there are a number of advantages to giving a free rendering of a story. In the first instance, a free rendering means that a teacher is not focused on a book: This allows more attention to be given to the children's reactions, to modulating her voice and to choosing appropriate language, perhaps incorporating gestures where appropriate. Furthermore, the sheer act of going to the trouble of learning a story off-by-heart can have a powerful effect, indicating to the listeners that the story is worthy of listening to. Lastly, free rendering of stories appears to be more effective in improving vocabulary development (Suggate, Lenhard et al., 2013), and is more engaging for children (Lenhart et al., 2018), especially if the content is fantasy-rich (Vaahtoranta et al., 2017; Weisberg et al., 2015). In comparison, there is evidence that young children learn very little, if any, language from screen media (Krcmar et al., 2007; Rosebury et al., 2009).

6.4 Rhythm, structure and security

Consciously implemented structure and rhythm requires effort, foresight and thought, all of which are activities closely linked to human 'I' or spiritual activity (see section 3.3). Recall also that for a child, their 'I' only manifests gradually, in phases (section 5.2.1). For this reason, well-selected and implemented rhythm and structure from the educators serve as a kind of 'I' for the child, reigning in more wild behaviours and providing reassurance and purpose. A wise educator can recognize two basic needs in children, which manifest as a kind of breathing in and breathing out (Nicol and Taplin, 2012). Breathing in refers to those times when children are engaged in more solitary, introverted or imaginative activities, providing time to withdraw from the external world and come more to themselves. In contrast, breathing out refers to activities in which more physical energy is expended; a child's focus is on more distal surroundings. In the following sections we refer to aspects of rhythm, structure and security adopted in Steiner education.

6.4.1 Experience of coherency

He who has a why to live, can bear almost any how.
(Friedrich Nietzsche)

Another area of emphasis in Waldorf-Steiner education is in demonstrating the coherency of individual processes – for example, how a plant grows from a seed, or how a toy is carved from a piece of wood. In today's technologically focused world, the opportunity to follow a process from beginning to end is increasingly rare. Although the mechanization of many daily processes may indeed increase efficiency, it becomes more and more difficult for children (and adults!) to understand how a process occurs. And despite many children's seemingly natural draw towards technological items, interactions with the multitude of electronic devices that abound are essentially abstract and very non-transparent (see section 8.3). When children manipulate the buttons on a dishwasher, they learn little about what is actually going on: they can press buttons and turn the machine on and off, perhaps are told 'not to touch the chemicals!', and are confronted by an array of beeps, until the cycle is finished and the dishes come out clean. In contrast, with a sink full of soapy, warm water, children receive a much richer sensory experience – feeling the warmth of the water, the bubbles, seeing the clear water slowly turning dull from the dirty dishes, and experiencing the satisfaction of dishes being clean through their own effort. Again, the difference in activation of children's wills is key.

The ability to perceive the coherency of processes can have an extraordinarily powerful effect on not only the psychological, but the physical health of a person. Among others, the psychiatrist Viktor Frankl illuminated how powerfully having a sense of purpose and coherency can work on adults (Frankl, 2008). Frankl's own experiences and observations during the Second World War brought him to the conclusion that – even under outwardly extremely difficult circumstances (for example, being in a concentration camp) – a sense of coherency, of purpose for why something is happening, can be protective towards maintaining physical and mental health.

In this light, Steiner educators endeavour to incorporate the principles of transparency, manageability, immediacy and coherency throughout the daily life of kindergarten. The Waldorf educator Peter Lang put it thus: Grind grain, bake bread, eat together, everything observable to the eye, in this way children can understand the world! (Compani, 2011, p. 44). As well as household tasks such as baking bread, gardening also offers a good opportunity for children to follow a process from one phase to the next, particularly in relation to the seasonal rhythms – after the snows of winter melt, new life starts to take hold again in spring. Living with the trusted, stable rhythms of nature may allow children to better discover their own place in the coherent whole.

6.4.2 Security and trust

Another important principle of Waldorf-Steiner education relates to creating a warm, secure environment, not without parallels to the experience of being in the womb (ibid.). The essence of the idea is that before children can actively

engage with their environments and develop healthily, they must first develop the trust that their own needs will be met: that is, that he or she is understood, and that the basic bodily needs (for example, warmth, nutritious food) are taken care of. Once a child trusts that these basic needs are met, he or she can begin to explore the environment around them. Such an 'anthroposophic' environment has been shown to be associated with lower levels of cortisol in children, which is indicative of lower levels of stress (Stenius et al., 2010).

6.4.3 Atmosphere

The younger the child, the more uncritically they absorb the impressions of the environment and the atmosphere in their surroundings, in part because their senses are less filtered and schooled than those of adults (see section 5.3). The way in which the room is organized also contributes to a feeling of security and warmth, and for this reason, there is an emphasis in Steiner kindergartens on the use of warm colours, sheep skins, blankets and cushions, as well as creating cosy corners and niches. Additionally, attention to the orderliness of the surroundings and, for example, expressions of gratitude, contribute to a feeling of both internal and external warmth and security. Perhaps the most important determinant of how comforting the environment feels, however, is dependent on the demeanour of the teachers. Steiner emphasized the importance of a genuine positive, upbeat mood and attitude around children (not to be confused, however, with a forced glib state – this is also inauthentic). Finally, it is important to note that children seem to be extremely sensitive to the emotional states of those in their environment, presumably also because they are somewhat more porous to their surroundings. Indeed, an environment that radiates warmth and authenticity creates the basis for a healthy trust in the teachers and the world around the child to develop.

6.4.4 An ordered environment

> The assistant was slowly and rhythmically cutting apples at her table… the teacher was weaving coloured wool on a wooden frame…. As they enter the kindergarten space, the children experience a sense of 'a place for everything and everything in its place' including the adults who are already steadily working at meaningful tasks.
>
> *(Drummond and Jenkinson, n.d., p. 26)*

Importantly, consideration is also given to creating a tidy, orderly environment in a Waldorf-Steiner kindergarten, whereby each individual toy and piece of equipment has its own place. The purpose of this practice is to help provide children with secure boundaries and security, and to help support their free play. Rather than interrupting the flow of play to search for a missing item or ask a teacher to find it, children can independently locate the desired play object. Instead of having all toys housed together in large toy boxes, each type of toy has its own home. For example, the dolls may be lying in prams, building blocks in their own box, coloured cloths may be found next to a basket of wool bands, and a basket of shells next to the container of chestnuts. Very quickly the children learn where objects belong, which also simplifies tidying up at the end of play time, allowing this to become a relatively independent activity. Furthermore, the teachers also repair any damaged toys, often with the help of the children. Our experience also suggests that toys are far more appealing to children when presented in this orderly, cared-for manner.

6.4.5 Rhythm and repetition

As mentioned, in addition to a secure attachment to the staff members in the kindergarten, the use of rhythm and repetition helps to cultivate the feeling of security, trust and equanimity. To the extent that each day, week and year is planned to incorporate a recognizable structure, the principles of rhythm and repetition can be viewed as essential to the education. In Steiner education, the word 'rhythm' is used here to indicate the recurring of similar situations, rather than a mechanical repetition of identical states. It is also interesting to note that when children are born, they possess little rhythm and little ability to regulate their own bodily processes. Digestion, day and night, sleeping and waking, and even breathing need to be learned, and become increasingly regulated.

Just as it is for an adult, beginning a new routine is a demanding exercise for a young child. At first, everything is new, and a great deal of energy is required to learn new names and faces, new tasks or games, words, and even to process the new details of the environment. With time, the new environment and people in it become familiar, and it is no longer as taxing. A child begins to recognize certain features and routines, and it becomes an almost automatic process to 'go through the motions' of the day. However, if there is little consistency from day to day, the child is constantly required to learn the routine anew, which can have an unsettling effect. The rhythm of the day and the week and the year provide the child with security, which allows him or her to better be able to experience the environment. Rather than needing to concentrate on whether it is now time to wash hands for the meal, or put shoes on to go outside, the child has more 'resources' to devote to, for example, the content of a story being told. Essentially, the experience of rhythm helps carry the child, freeing his or her feet for other activities. Furthermore, it is a very satisfying experience as a child (or as an adult!) to recognize a routine or a song and be able to participate fully. Each time children hear the same story, a different aspect may resonate with them.

Even though a child may not know the hour on the clock, they can begin to trust that after playing in the garden, it is time to go home. In this sense, the actual length of time spent doing a given activity is perhaps less important than the maintenance of the pattern of the day. Rather than sticking rigidly to an hourly time structure, the individual needs of the group of children on a given day are considered and altered accordingly. For example, the period of time spent in the garden may well be shorter during the winter, but it will always occur, for example, after the meal, and before the story-time.

Incidentally, not only is the familiar daily, weekly or yearly structure of the day reassuring for the children, it is also particularly helpful for the kindergarten teachers themselves. Once a rhythm or ritual becomes established, it provides the necessary structure for the teaching staff to feel comfortable about the next step of the day, rather than being preoccupied with wondering what on earth to do next! In turn, the resulting calmness typically further positively improves the atmosphere of the group. On the other hand, when neither the children nor the teachers are sure as to the next steps, the situation can very quickly spiral out of control.

As a result, conscious attention is given to strengthening rhythm and repetition in the form of reoccurring daily, weekly and yearly activities, songs and rituals (see also section 7.3 for more specific examples of the rhythms employed in a Waldorf-Steiner kindergarten).

6.4.6 Ceremony and ritual

Rituals in Steiner kindergartens perform the function of easing transition phases between activities, as well as helping create an inviting and calming mood. They provide an indirect indication to children that it is time to finish their current activity and that a new activity will soon begin. The rituals in Waldorf-Steiner kindergartens are sometimes very simple – for example, the ringing of a small bell to indicate it is time to begin tidying up, or lighting a candle to indicate it is time to be quiet and still (for example, before a meal time or a story). Often the children themselves play a role in these rituals, by taking turns to ring the bell or blow out the match used to light the candle. Such rituals help create a familiar structure, which provides security for many children.

Another common ritual found in many Steiner kindergartens after hand-washing is the 'drop of golden oil' ritual, whereby a teacher or child goes around the circle of children with a small dish of oil, putting a drop of this oil in each child's waiting hands. This ritual is accompanied by a song, and each child waits expectantly for their often rose-scented drop, before rubbing it into their hands and smelling the essential oils. This ritual is a subtle sense experience and has a very calming effect, allowing children a few moments of peace and the opportunity to 'reconnect with themselves' before moving on to the next activity.

6.5 Whole nutrition

> A food is all the more a sustaining source of life, to the extent that it contains forces of life and to the extent that these are not destroyed during preparation.
>
> *(Wolff, 2012, p. 31, authors' translation)*

The importance of food in society the world over is manifold. Not only is food a necessity of life, it is often a decidedly social activity, with many people's fondest memories formed around a table with friends or family. Just as through culture, rocks, dust and ash give rise to cathedrals, theatres and works of art, so too can humble grains of food be raised to a higher level through the right preparation and the right mood. Imagine a carefully laid table, with a candle and a vase of freshly cut spring flowers in the middle, plates, cups and serviettes neatly arranged at each place. Sharing a meal is about more than simply satiating hunger: it is a communal activity, a ceremony.

In Waldorf kindergartens, each meal begins with a short blessing and lighting of a candle, which helps to create an air of reverence and gratitude for the meal. Children are typically involved in the dishing out of food and drinks; and once every child (and adult) has their meal, all children begin to eat at the same time. There may be a thoughtful air of concentration, or quiet chatter between the children, depending on the kindergarten.

Before discussing the effects of various food types on the human organism, it is worth considering the purpose of eating. Although many people view food consumption as either a means of enjoyment or simply a way of ingesting sufficient calories in order to perform the tasks required of them, nutrition can also be seen as a way of stimulating life itself (ibid., p. 31). If we take this view as our starting point, it becomes clear that the more 'life' a given food product contains when we consume it, the more life it is likely to be able to pass on to us as those consuming the food.

6.5.1 Participative food preparation

Being the natural imitators that they are, it is only a matter of time before most children ask to help in the kitchen. Although the meal preparation naturally takes somewhat longer with little helpers, there are a number of benefits to involving children. First of all, it allows them to follow a process from beginning to end (see section 6.4.1), which is a distinctly satisfying experience. Secondly, they gradually develop a broad array of food preparation skills that will stand them in good stead for their later lives – as an adult, the task of cooking a meal from scratch is not nearly so overwhelming when you have always helped in the kitchen, and you know that food does not necessarily just come from a packet. And thirdly, many children are actually more likely to try novel foods if they themselves

have been involved in the preparation. Given the alarming increase in illnesses such as obesity and Type II diabetes (Dabelea et al., 2014; Ebbeling et al., 2002), there is reason to believe that improved awareness of the foundations of a healthy diet from childhood onwards is vitally important.

6.5.2 Nature's bounty

> The failure to maintain a healthy agriculture has largely cancelled out all the advantages we have gained from improvements in hygiene, in housing, and medical discoveries.
>
> *(Sir Albert Howard, 1945, founder of the Soil Association; cited Soil Association, 2001)*

Nature's bounty is to be enjoyed and contributed to through care for the earth. In this section we look at four aspects of this bounty that have immediate educational implications – namely, the senses, seasonality, variety and organic preparation.

Sweet, sour, bitter, runny, lumpy, smooth… sense impressions abound in the eating and harvesting of food. Interacting with a variety of different foods allows young children to discover many different flavours, textures, smells and colours, and, as such, provides many rich sensory experiences (see also Chapter 3). Indeed, phenomenologically our sense impressions actually betray the inner nature of a food, and help us to develop a better understanding of

the effect of a given food. One very clear example is that of poisonous foods, for example, certain berries – they are typically very bitter, which instantly alerts us to the fact that this food is probably not fit for our consumption. Additionally, the taste for healthy food also becomes almost habitual. Adults tend to prefer food that they ate as children, so kindergarten provides an opportunity to set healthy eating on the right path.

Wherever possible, it is desirable to eat in line with the seasons. Levels of digestive enzymes have actually been shown to change across the course of the year. For example, the enzyme amylase – necessary for the digestion of starch, including wheat – rises during the winter months, before falling again in spring and summer (Douillard, 2017). Given that wheat is traditionally harvested in autumn, this allows for better digestion of a seasonal product. In fact, in one traditional hunter-gatherer tribe in Tanzania, evidence has been found of a changing gut microbiome in rhythm with the changing seasons, with more enzymes for digesting animal starches in the dry season, and more enzymes for digesting plant starches in the rainy season (Smits et al., 2017). There are also obvious social and environmental reasons for eating with the seasons, such as supporting local producers and reducing pollution arising from transport.

Interestingly, in the modern day and age where there is a desire to isolate minerals and vitamins to supplement most exactly, there is evidence to suggest that various components of a food – even those that at first pass appear to be inessential – work together to make that food nutritious. This can be termed 'food synergy' (Jacobs and Steffen, 2003). The lesson here is that variety is important. The biochemistry of food is exceptionally complex, and this is only one level of analysis. New constituents are constantly being discovered (e.g. anti-oxidants, essential fatty acids, vitamins); however, the message remains the same – both too much or too little of one food is usually detrimental.

In Waldorf-Steiner kindergartens, an emphasis is placed on the use of organic, and where possible, biodynamic produce. In organic – and to an even greater extent biodynamic – agriculture, the earth is viewed as more than a mere medium for producing as much produce as possible, but rather as a living organism. As a result, organic and biodynamic produce is not fertilized by artificial means, nor treated with herbicides or pesticides, with techniques such as crop rotation, crop diversification and the use of composts used instead (Reganold, 1995). The major difference between biodynamic and organic agriculture is the use of eight specific plant or animal-based preparations in the biodynamic approach. Additionally, other requirements exist, such as producing 50 per cent of livestock feed on the farm, rather than buying it in, with a higher degree of self-sufficiency than expected on organic farms (Schreier and Association Soin de la Terre, 2015).

The dangers of chemical fertilizers not only to the environment but to humans too are now well known (Soil Association, 2001). For example, the problematic nature of nitrates, which are particularly associated with run-off from intensive farming, is becoming increasingly recognized. Babies who drink water contaminated with nitrates can become very unwell, sometimes even turning blue, and they may go into a coma or die if not treated promptly (e.g. Knobeloch et al., 2000). It is not only babies who are susceptible, however – high rates of nitrates have also been associated with certain types of cancers (ibid.). Furthermore, as nitrates have the effect of stimulating growth, often unnaturally quickly, the effect appears to be that foods high in nitrates are also less nutritious and have poorer flavour.

There is evidence that both biodynamic and organic agriculture are associated with better soil quality. For example, biodynamic farms were found to have more earthworms per square metre, as well as higher amounts of organic soil matter and topsoil, when compared with conventional farms (Reganold et al., 1993). Specifically, as a proportion of soil mass, one study found that biodynamic farms had an average of 86.3g of earthworms per square metre compared with only 3.4g of earthworms per square metre in conventional farming soil (ibid.). There is also an indication that biodynamic preparations improve crop yields in some cases, as well as reducing storage losses (Goldstein, 2000).

6.5.3 Digestion as an activity

> Life is light, transformed.
> *(Wolff, 2012, p. 16)*

Whereas in decades and centuries gone by, under-nourishment and a lack of food were commonplace, these days in the Western world, we typically suffer from an overabundance of food available for our consumption (although this does not necessarily mean we are better nourished!). Unlike animals, human beings not only eat to satiate themselves but also as a form of enjoyment; and coupled with a ready abundance of food, this has actually led to the advent of illnesses that were previously unknown, such as gout and various liver and digestion problems (Wolff, 2007, pp. 25–6). As such, more awareness needs to be given to the process of digestion.

In particular, the importance of rhythm with regard to eating patterns is worthy of consideration (see also section 5.5). As with many other practices in Waldorf kindergartens, meals too have a familiar pattern to them, both in terms of the food served and the time at which it is served. The meal, for example, may be held at 10 o'clock, with no snacking before or after this time. This is to help children's bodies develop a natural rhythm, whereby their digestive organs are at work and then at rest, rather than being constantly confronted with food that requires digesting. Furthermore, breaks between meals are important for the health of our teeth, in order to allow our mouth saliva to regulate the pH in our mouths and help prevent cavities.

Rhythm also flows into the weekly meal plans, in which most kindergartens have a rotating schedule, with a particular food being associated with a particular day of the week (see section 6.3). Sometimes meals based on a different grain are served each day, or sometimes different methods of preparation distinguish the days, such as soup day, or bread day. Some kindergartens may even vary the colour of foods served on a given day of the week (Hildreth, 2006).

As with many areas of life, finding the appropriate balance between stimulating the digestive processes too much and too little is important. A sluggish digestive system tends to result in constipation, and an overactive digestive system may result in diarrhoea, whereas a healthy digestive system has the ability to break food down to a sufficient degree that the greatest nutritional value can be extracted from it. In short, highly processed foods (as well as perhaps introducing unwanted chemicals into the body) also rob the digestive system of the opportunity to work and, through these efforts, strengthen itself. A well-functioning digestive system is also important for avoiding food allergies, as such allergies are often the result of the body's inability to handle undigested protein, which can occur if the digestive organs are functioning poorly (Wolff, 1988). Furthermore, from an anthroposophical viewpoint a well-functioning digestive system allows each element of the child to flourish, improving general health and well-being.

6.5.4 Some key foods under the microscope

> In recent times, our expectations have completely changed: Each and everyone feels himself to be a 'king' such that all culinary delights should be available, at all times, with as little effort as possible.
> *(Wolff, 2012, p. 68, authors' translation)*

The effects of sugar on children can be well observed by attending a children's birthday party and watching the hyperactivity that ensues as the children fill up on sweets, cakes and fizzy drinks! It is no wonder – the sugar has just provided the children with an instant energy boost, and the excess energy needs to find its way out. But the trouble with excess amounts of sugar is that they place strain on the liver and the pancreas, which is responsible for producing insulin to return blood sugar to an appropriate level. If the sugar that has just been ingested cannot be readily utilized by the body in the form of activity, then this 'excess energy' is laid down as fat reserves. For this reason, the consumption of large amounts of sugar is intimately connected with the dramatic rise of excess weight, obesity and diabetes in children. And what constitutes an excessive amount of sugar? The World Health Organization recommends that children consume no more than 15g (three teaspoons) of sugar per day. A quick look at the back of some common food products – be they 'treats' or otherwise – confirms that these three teaspoons are quickly reached with only one chocolate bar, or one can of fizzy drink – and sometimes even with only one bowl of children's breakfast cereal.

As Otto Wolff puts it, sugar is an 'energy source without life' (2012). It does not contain any vitamins itself, and actually robs the body of vitamin B for its digestion (Wolff, 2012, p. 48). Additionally, as insulin cleans up the excess blood sugar, there is an energy drop that predictably follows the initial energy high – the result of which has many people reaching for more sugar to stave of this energy dip. Importantly, it is worth mentioning at this point that although refined white sugar is certainly detrimental in this regard, other forms of sugar, even more natural sugars such as maple syrup, coconut sugar or fruit juice, also have this effect. Furthermore, simple starches, such as products made from white flour or white rice, are also subject to this phenomenon.

As with sugar, the digestion of wheat requires vitamin B which, fortuitously, is found in the husk of the grain itself. However, if one consumes highly processed wheat – where the husk has been removed to create a finer, more palatable product – the problem described above, of taxing the body's vitamin B stores, can also be seen. As wheat is now, without competition, the most widely consumed grain in the world (Wolff, 2012), it is worth looking a little more closely at this ubiquitous product.

There are a number of issues to consider. First of all, the amount of wheat that is being eaten has increased dramatically in the last century. In 1893 Germany, for example, people were eating twice as much rye as they were wheat. By the year 1970, Germans were now eating three times as much wheat as rye (Wolff, 2012), and there is reason to believe that the proportional consumption of wheat has increased further still since 1970, and is perhaps even more common in the English-speaking world than in Germany. Interestingly, wheat is referred to in the old testament by way of the description 'fine flour' (Leviticus 24: 5–9) as being reserved for special ceremonies and rituals, and as such, was previously used more judiciously, for special occasions and the like (Wolff, 2012).

Secondly, the type of wheat which is now consumed is almost exclusively high-gluten wheat. Gluten is a protein that provides the elastic quality of wheat products. As mentioned above, when protein is not properly broken down, allergies begin to occur, and this high-gluten wheat seems to be straining our digestive capabilities. This may help explain why rates of gluten intolerance and sensitivities seem to be rising dramatically.

Thirdly, the way in which wheat is prepared can be problematic. Whereas traditional bread products were produced using a fermented sourdough, the vast majority of bread products today are leavened with yeast. Interestingly, the breakdown of sourdough in the body results in milk acids, which are natural metabolites; but in contrast, the breakdown of yeast results in carbon dioxide and alcohol (Wolff, 2012). According to Wolff (ibid.), although this alcohol is practically eliminated during the baking process, it remains the case that the metabolic breakdown of yeast is essentially 'foreign' to our bodies.

As with sugar and wheat, the consumption of milk products, especially in the form of pure milk, has increased considerably in recent decades. And as with wheat, this contrasts with more traditional consumption of milk products in the form of products like yoghurt or quark. The process of fermentation can essentially be considered a type of pre-digestion, which explains why fermented milk products are typically more easily digested generally, and especially by those with sensitivities. The fact that more and more people are presenting with sensitivities and allergies to both milk and wheat (ibid., p. 67) begs the question as to whether our changing diets may be contributing to this development.

Of course, nutrition is an exceedingly complicated topic, and new understanding and revelations are constantly coming to light. It is important to mention that the above considerations are presented here by way of descriptions of the qualities of a few common food products, rather than hard-and-fast rules. To omit all of the above food groups from one's diet would not only lead to estrangement from the world, it may very well not be healthy. However, particularly in an age of rampant food allergies and other chronic health conditions – starting at younger and younger ages – being aware of the effects of certain food types can allow us to moderate our consumption where required, or make different choices (for example, to choose a soured milk or bread product). And as Otto Wolff maintains, a food that may be harmful for one person may be necessary for the next (Wolff, 2007).

6.6 Relating to the child

Naturally the art of teaching involves being able to relate to many different types of children, and having the sensitivity to determine the needs of a given child in a given moment. Although there are few hard-and-fast rules, and certainly nothing can replace the wealth of knowledge gained by working and interacting with different children over many years, there are a few guidelines that can help in the development of a secure, trusting relationship between child and teacher, and maintaining a happy, healthy classroom environment. Notably, some of the techniques used by the Waldorf-Steiner kindergarten teacher may initially appear quite foreign to those of a conventionally trained educator.

6.6.1 Establishing a meaningful relationship with the child

The relationship between the children and the staff has a tremendous impact on the quality of a kindergarten, and provides a secure base from which a child can go into the world (Lang, 2011). In much the same way as a young toddler just starting to walk often returns to his or her mother or father to check that they are still there and to receive encouragement, children new to kindergarten need to feel trust in their teachers to provide this security and feeling of protection. As such, particular importance is placed upon interacting with the child in such a way that he or she feels understood.

Taking an interest in that which interests the child, and attempting to perceive and understand the child's current state, help develop trust and allow the

child to fully engage in the environment. Engaging with the child, perhaps sharing a joke, crafting, or singing a song together are all forms of positive interaction (rather than negative interaction, such as reprimanding) that help foster respect and interest. A healthy, open relationship with the parents and the family is also an important basis on which to build a trusting relationship between teacher and child (Compani, 2011); for if the parents have misgivings, it is likely that the child will pick up on this on some level, and then struggle to settle into the kindergarten environment. Perhaps most important of all in developing a meaningful relationship with the child is that the teacher be authentic. When a teacher remains true to his or her word, is consistent and speaks the truth, this is generally a very solid basis upon which to build a trusting relationship.

6.6.2 Interacting with the child

When a child arrives at kindergarten at the start of the day, he or she is welcomed by the teacher, perhaps with a shake of the hand, a rub on the back, a smile or a few words of greeting. Children are very unlikely to be peppered with questions about how they are feeling, or what they did on the weekend: rather, they are left free to join in with an activity, sit in the doll's corner, or simply observe what is going on.

It is often observed by those unfamiliar with Steiner early child education that compared to other early childhood environments, the kindergarten teachers assume more of a background role in the classroom, at least on the surface. In one instance, a visitor to a Steiner kindergarten is observed to seemingly compensate for the kindergarten teacher when she leaves the room, by asking a group of children who are drawing, questions about their favourite colours, and praising the pictures (Drummond, 2011). It is noted that the air of quiet application that was present when the Steiner teacher was in the room was replaced by a frenetic competing for the visitor's attention.

This example serves to illustrate a few key characteristics of a Steiner teacher's interaction with the children. She typically asks very few questions of the children, preferring to leave them absorbed in their world of play. One Steiner teacher commented that, 'If you are watching the children, it means they become more self-conscious, and they won't play in the same way... the more engaged the teacher is with what he or she is doing, the more engaged the children are in their play...' (Drummond and Jenkinson, n.d., p. 20). Similarly, when a child is helpful, the teacher is most unlikely to say 'What a fantastic helper you are!', preferring to acknowledge the gesture with a quiet, appreciative smile and a 'thank you'.

Additionally, when children do ask questions of the teachers, the attempt is to answer them in a straightforward, non-intellectual way (see also section 5.2.2). Children's questions can sometimes be answered by helping them to better observe the process themselves (e.g. operating a manual apple press, baking bread by hand). Essentially, though, the aim is not to provide children with an answer that will go over their heads, or unduly tax their intellectual faculties, but one that captures an air of wonder.

6.6.3 Discipline

In their book *Understanding the Steiner Waldorf Approach*, Nicol and Taplin (2012) talk about using 'creative discipline' (pp. 77–79). Essentially, the approach in a Steiner kindergarten tends to vary with the age of the child. Distraction is often the most appropriate technique with young children, who are generally just as happy engaged in helping the teacher set the table as they previously were in knocking down another child's tower of blocks. Another creative approach they suggest using is redirecting a game that may be becoming dangerous – for example, when a heavy log of wood is being wielded as a hairdryer. By providing a basket of pegs and saying 'It is time for the curling tongs now, let me put that hairdryer back into the storeroom' (p. 78), the flow of play is not interrupted, but the potentially dangerous item is removed from play. Similarly, a well-timed song or finger game can reset the mood in the group or lower noise levels, without having to resort to directives like 'Quiet, please'.

Nicol and Taplin (2012) also recognize that it may be necessary to have a child stay close to an adult, if that child is repeatedly hurting other children, or being otherwise aggressive or socially inappropriate. This method can be implemented in a matter-of-fact way, without even raising one's voice, but must be responded to for the health of the group and before such behaviour becomes modelled by other children.

Another aspect of what may be broadly termed 'discipline' can simply be drawing a child's attention to the consequences of their actions. For example, if a child is fooling around and places a cup precariously on the edge of the table and it gets knocked to the floor and breaks, there is a natural consequence to this action – namely, that the breakage needs clearing up. Similarly, a child may push another child and knock them over, creating the natural consequence that the hurt child needs comforting, or perhaps treating. By involving the child in attending to these consequences, for example 'Could you please bring me the dustpan and broom / a plaster?', the child has an opportunity to learn from his or her actions.

A long-term creative approach to discipline can also be achieved through story-telling (Nicol and Taplin, 2012). Telling the whole group, say, a fairy tale in which a good, honest princess triumphs over a wicked wizard can have the effect of subtly modifying the behaviour of the whole group – but particularly those who are struggling socially – over the course of many months. Finally, having a few basic rules that are clear for all children – with regard to respecting one another, property and sharing – can help alleviate many problems before they eventuate. As always, it is important that the teachers, as prominent role models, also adhere to these rules!

In general, having a wide repertoire of songs, rhymes, verses, finger games, activities and stories is absolutely invaluable. The right song or rhyme at the right time can have a magical effect: it can calm or enthuse, it can spur children into action or encourage them to come to rest, it can even help resolve disputes. To observe a rowdy bunch of children becoming as quiet as mice with the aid of a finger game is a wonder to behold!

6.6.4 Purposeful activity

> They see adults washing clothes, making bread, chopping vegetables, and digging the garden, things that make sense to them. … And purposeful adults create purposeful play, because the children are imitators… and play is a serious business to a child.
>
> *(Drummond and Jenkinson, n.d., p. 20)*

Aside from the obvious expectations of the teacher in kindergarten, to respond to the needs of the children in their care, and ensure they are safe and their emotional needs are met, there are a number of further roles of a Steiner early-childhood teacher. They are also responsible for ensuring a tidy, attractive environment and, most importantly, for remaining cognizant of their position as a role model for children, and hence engaging in behaviour that is worthy of imitation.

To this end, teachers try to remain purposefully busy, which in its simplest sense involves ensuring that the necessary tasks are completed to allow a smooth daily routine to progress. This important work has been termed the 'domestic arts' (Nicol, 2011). This involves preparing meals, washing dishes, preparing for the various festivals and tending to the gardening. Additionally, to the extent that each teacher has an interest in and is capable of doing so, teachers often busy themselves with handcrafts or other similar aesthetic activities. For example, the teachers may play an instrument, paint, weave or work on a woodcarving project – essentially a wide range of activities that children enjoy observing, getting involved with or potentially imitating in their own play. Even the most menial of tasks can be enjoyable, and the art of the Waldorf early childhood teacher is to allow an interest in life to permeate his or her every move.

6.7 Self-development and reflection

> Compare and contrast: a small group of quiet, focused teachers, thinking together, by the light of a candle – and a mainstream educator, sitting down, probably alone, with paper and pen, to complete the 17 nine-point scales of the Early Years Foundation Stage Profile. It is hard to imagine two more different scenarios.
> *(Drummond and Jenkinson, n.d., p. 39)*

As the starting point in considering the importance of teachers' self-development in Steiner education, consider the following exercise. Imagine two kindergartens with the same daily routine, the teachers have the same number of years of experience, the rooms are identical, the same trees bestow the children with their grace and protection in the garden outside, and the same natural materials – toys, nutrition, furniture, crayons, candles – are equally abundant. There is one key difference, however: the teachers in the one kindergarten reflect daily on the broader purpose of their work, their own faults, and the children in their care are seen as gifts to be unwrapped, or riddles to be partly solved, to be helped on their long journey. In the other kindergarten, a good deal of thought is given to the children too, but more on a practical level; how to manage children, what logistically is needed for the next day, what behavioural disorders might be present and so on. Would these two kindergartens be experienced as being identical by children, teachers and parents? We maintain, also out of experience from visiting many different kindergartens, that the answer to this hypothetical question is a clear 'no'. There is simply something present weaving its way through the actions of the teachers, permeating the very fabric of the room. This aesthetic-protective force is harnessed through, and arises out of, the work that the teachers do on themselves. This work we divide into the work that adults do on themselves, and the work that directly concerns the children.

6.7.1 Teacher self-development

Throughout this book, we repeatedly refer to a holistic, phenomenological view of humanity. According to this view, it is difficult to separate the observer from the observed, the actors from the enacted (Seamon and Zajonc, 1998). If one combines this understanding with children's spectacular ability to imitate (see section 6.1), it follows that kindergarten teachers need to develop themselves to help children develop. However, self-development is complex; it has about as many different forms as there are individual human beings, not the least of which because self-development needs to be consciously adopted in freedom by each human 'I'. This makes it clear that the commitment to conscious or even accelerated self-development – because self-development occurs constantly, whether we try to actively engage in it or not – touches upon an inner sanctum. No institution or other individual can or should exert any pressure on kindergarten teachers to this extent.

However, a good deal can be achieved towards deepening educational understanding by developing a culture of self-development and critical reflection. The most simple to describe, yet ironically sometimes the most difficult to enact – especially under pressure – refers to simple decency in the way in which adults interact with one another. This includes basic aspects of behaviour such as honesty and tact, being able to talk to each other, not about each other. Other important aspects are reliability, fairness, balance, open-mindedness and the effort to try to understand what another person is conveying, not necessarily simply what he or she actually says. Steiner provided many exercises that school these facets of behaviour, in particular the so-called subsidiary exercises, or the weekly practice of moral qualities (Steiner, 1998). The opening chapters of his book *How To Know Higher Worlds* (Steiner, 1919/2008) are also inspiring, gently elucidating the heart-warming morality of practising basic human decency. In our age of networking and accruing approval from others, such works and thoughts centre and ground us to what is truly essential. The practice of these qualities can lead to a peacefulness, gratitude and purpose in daily life, which is, in turn, highly beneficial for the kindergarten.

Parallel to developing a culture of openness and reflection, Steiner teachers often also meet, if possible weekly, to study an educational text, usually from Steiner's writings. Steiner's texts are often written in such a way that one is constantly being needled and surprised, with the same phenomenon viewed from many sides. This creates a series of questions, moments of inner resistance and reconciliation; in short, one is prompted to constantly reflect. Such activity, which also requires much concentration, serves to invigorate the soul-life. His works are often not written in the easily digestible manner of modern prose[18] but instead require inner activity. For this reason, it is beneficial for kindergarten teachers to not only study Steiner's educational texts, but also his other works (e.g. philosophy, cosmology, religion, arts, architecture, agriculture, medicine etc.). Of course, we also encourage kindergarten teachers to study literature from other approaches and disciplines: doing so is important for both learning and broadening horizons, as well as realising ever anew what is unique about the Steiner approach (see section 7.6).

A third way in which teachers can engage in self-development is through actively participating in meditation. Meditation has become a popular term as a result of the adoption of Eastern religions in the West, and also through its increasing use in psychotherapy (i.e. mindfulness) as a means of relaxing and coming to a state of acceptance. Steiner's meditations, however, are qualitatively different: for him, extinguishing the content of consciousness to reach a higher plane is neither desirable nor possible. Consciousness is always present in one form or another; the question is, how active in my conscious experience am I? His exercises focus on developing aspects of ourselves that are normally dormant or aberrant, rendering us broader and more balanced. Steiner's meditations focus not so much on acceptance of the world, but rather on acceptance of the unchangeable parts of the world and tireless courage to use this life to help the world progress where possible.

Meditation in this sense is not, therefore, about reaching higher states of consciousness as a primary goal, but about helping the world evolve, which may or may not require us reaching a higher state of consciousness. It should be emphasized again that such activity falls exclusively in the free and autonomous domain of each adult – it belongs to freehood, not to institutional or social pressure. Of course, the danger in self-development is also one of self-delusion. Alongside suggestions given by Steiner in the form of subsidiary exercises (Steiner, 1998), he saw nothing more important than standing firmly in life, while endeavouring to greet all that there is in the world with the greatest possible openness. In short, for the kindergarten teacher there is no replacement for getting one's hands dirty through practical work, listening patiently to the concerns of parents and colleagues, and 'forgetting' oneself through devotion to the children in one's care.

6.7.2 Understanding children

To understand children, one also has to understand oneself, as well as the effects we have on children in our care. Steiner pointed out how words and deeds affect children's physiology, penetrating right down into the organism and rhythmic system of the child (Steiner, 1996b). We know from physiological parameters that heart rate, cortisol levels and breathing changes depend on the emotional activity of adults. Parents often experience that when they themselves are stressed – seemingly regardless of how well they disguise this – children act differently. Recognizing our own states and their effect on children is the first step towards understanding children.

From a phenomenological perspective, to better understand a child also requires understanding the influence of the external world in all its complexity. Viewing the external conditions of children's lives often allows a little more understanding of the inner nature of each child. For this reason, many kindergartens conduct home visits in which the teachers visit the child and family at their home. This also has the advantage of strengthening the relationship, with the children feeling that their parents are behind the teachers and vice versa.

6.7.2.1 Child conferences and child studies

Child conferences or child studies are used in Steiner kindergartens as an important means to better understand children (Jenkinson, 2011). In these meetings, depending on the institution, each child is typically the subject of a kindergarten conference once or twice a year. Specifically, one teacher might describe a child from her or his group to the other teachers, trying to present a picture that is as living and characteristic as possible. The teacher tries to avoid making judgements because these work counter to developing a clear picture. Personal likes or dislikes are also cast aside, with all the teachers describing how they perceive the child. The child is, figuratively speaking, placed in the room like a piece of art work and given full attention. Even at the end of the exercise, it is important that judgements are not formed, but rather that the teachers leave with a more rounded picture than they had before they entered the meeting. Then the image is taken into sleep and perhaps continued at another child conference. Teachers who regularly engage in this practice swear by its importance, often reporting that not only does their own understanding grow through this process, but also that the child often changes too (Drummond and Jenkinson, n.d.). It could be, for instance, that the child had previously had difficulty making friends, or disrupted story-time; yet often the very next day, the child can behave differently, without the teachers having actually changed anything other than their own perspective.

In a Nutshell

- Educating to freehood requires working with children's development out of an understanding of the whole human being.

- In the early years, educators can capitalize on children's drive to imitate as an educational principle.

- Free play, artistic activities, sense-rich play materials and mindful language can be used to guide and unfold children's imaginations.

- Rhythm, structure, security, orderly surroundings, aesthetic activities and atmosphere work in a soothing and supporting way on the developing child.

- Appropriate nutrition and participative food preparation derived from nature's bounty constitute important developmental factors.

- Meaningful relationships characterized by purposeful activity and deep perception and self-reflection imbue the kindergarten culture in a benevolent manner.

CHAPTER 7

Steiner Education in Practice

The actual practice of Steiner education is derived from the previously described principles and underlying understanding of children, childhood and the role of education. How this is practically realised varies from kindergarten to kindergarten, state to state, country to country, and culture to culture. Despite this necessary and desirable variation, there are also many similarities, such that one can quite quickly recognize that one is in a Steiner institution, be it in Brazil or Kenya. The purpose of this chapter is to outline some of the specific elements of this practice and then compare it to other approaches.

7.1 The historical development of Waldorf-Steiner

Childcare facilities for large groups of preschool-aged children came into existence during the late eighteenth century, but Friedrich Fröbel is commonly credited with founding the first 'children's gardens' (or kindergartens) in southern Germany in 1837. Fröbel's kindergartens were intended to raise children like plants, with tender care, and they emphasized the importance of music, story-telling and play. Disciples of his went into the world and were responsible for starting many German-language kindergartens in America, inspiring Elizabeth Peabody to open the first English-speaking kindergarten in 1860. In England, Samuel Wilderspin, who opened his first infant school in 1819, also advocated a focus on play. Margaret McMillan was a forerunner in the development of nursery schools, and was also a contemporary of Steiner's, having helped organize Steiner's 1923 lecture cycle in England.

Although the first lasting Waldorf kindergarten was founded in early 1926, a year after Steiner's death, the pedagogical principles that provide the foundation for the movement had been presented by Steiner in various lecture courses, particularly in *The Foundations of Human Experience* (Steiner, 1996b). On Steiner's request, Elisabeth von Grunelius was charged with the task of setting up the first Waldorf kindergarten.

Despite the claim that Rudolf Steiner was never in favour of the establishment of Waldorf kindergartens, the first kindergarten actually opened before his death, in 1920, but was forced to close again a short time later due to space and financial constraints (von Grunelius, 1993). Steiner also commented during a lecture that it was unfortunate that children in the highly imitative first seven years of life did not come into contact with Steiner education (von Kügelgen, 1993), also serving to suggest that he too saw a place for Steiner kindergartens in society. In fact, in a round of lectures that were later published in *Soul Economy and Waldorf Education*, he said '…it grieves me deeply that our Waldorf school in Stuttgart can accept only children who have reached the official school age, and it would give me the greatest satisfaction if we could take in the younger children as well' (2003, p. 101).

Certainly, however, the initial ideas and indications given by Steiner have required much further development, and the Waldorf kindergarten movement has grown considerably since the mid-1920s. Prior to the Second World War, a further few kindergartens opened in Germany (von Kügelgen, 1993), but at least externally, the movement was halted in Germany during the war years due to the Nazis banning Waldorf schools from running. In 1940, Elisabeth von Grunelius, who had continued to run the original kindergarten until 1938, was invited to go to America, where she was responsible for helping to establish the first American Waldorf kindergarten in Kimberton, and then a second on Long Island in 1948. In 1954, she returned to European shores, where she was involved in founding a new kindergarten in Paris.

In the mean time, after the end of the Second World War, the Waldorf kindergarten movement again blossomed. In 1969, the Association of Waldorf Kindergartens was founded, allowing greater communication between countries, support for new kindergartens, and continued development and training of teachers (von Kügelgen, 1993). By April 2018 there were nearly 1,900 Waldorf kindergartens around the world (Bund der Freien Waldorfschulen, 2018). However, it is important to mention that although Steiner's impulse and indications provide a solid foundation for the Waldorf kindergarten movement, this naturally needs to be continually augmented with careful consideration and observation of children by well-trained Waldorf kindergarten teachers. Only in this way can teachers be sure that they are best meeting the needs of the children in their care, as they present today (see section 8.4).

7.2 A typical setting: The environment as the third teacher

> The younger the children, the less they can free themselves from
> dependence upon their environment. Even though they receive
> their strongest impressions from people, whether adults or children,
> everything surrounding them contributes in one way or another
> to their development, and this fact calls for special care in the
> arrangement of a kindergarten setting.
>
> *(von Grunelius, 1950/1991, p. 32).*

The overriding consideration in the design – both inside and out – is how best
to protect the natural state of wonder and openness in young children. On
the one hand, this mood of soul enables young children to readily imitate and
learn from their environment. On the other hand, however, this openness,
coupled with a less developed ability to filter their environment, means
they are more sensitive to the influences and impressions around them than
are adults. In fact, as the external and internal worlds of a child are little
differentiated, Steiner actually considered that a child was essentially a sense
organ (Selg, 2017). For this reason, careful attention is given to how a room
is presented and arranged, down to the level of the play materials, and as such
the kindergarten room is considered to be the 'third educator' (as is also the
case with other education approaches; see section 7.6).

The architecture of Waldorf kindergartens constitutes a unique element of
the education. The guiding principle is the attempt to create cohesion and

harmony between the building and its surroundings, such that the building appears to 'grow' organically out of its environment, rather than stand apart from it. In this respect, much of the inspiration for such a building style comes from the Goetheanum in Dornach, Switzerland. In particular, there is an emphasis placed on using more naturally occurring geometric forms, with few straight lines, and proportions such as would be found in nature. The external design is intended to be welcoming and inviting, without overwhelming the children – instead creating corners and niches to which the eye can wander.

Nearly every Waldorf kindergarten also has an outside area, which is based on the same design principles of creating an inviting environment without being overwhelming. Additionally, the outdoor area should offer opportunities for free play and exertion, letting off steam and trialling new activities, as well as the possibility of engaging in meaningful activity (von Grunelius, 1950/1991). To meet these requirements, most kindergartens have not only structured areas like flower beds, sand pits and swings, but also naturally occurring areas allowing varied sensory experiences and exploration. For example, there may be bushes, shrubs and vines for hiding in or collecting berries, shady areas under trees and sunny patches of grass, as well as more hilly, untamed spots. For those children who would like to help tend the gardens, there are child-sized tools, as well as spades and sand toys.

The design of indoor spaces is marked by a harmonious flow of peaceful, quiet areas into move active, engaging areas. The kindergarten rooms are typically organized with a large, open space allowing ample room to build and move, as well as more protected play corners and separate rooms for sleeping. Additionally, there is invariably also a small kitchen in which children can actively participate in or observe the meal preparation.

Furthermore, particular detail is also paid to the choice of colours and furniture used in the decoration. Great care is taken to ensure that the right mood is created using particular colours, cloths, carved wooden furniture and natural daylight. The walls are typically painted in warm pinks and yellows using a special technique, such that the colours flow naturally into one another. In the words of Elizabeth von Grunelius:

> Plain light colours without wallpaper designs, which after a time
> become tiresome for the live imagination, provide a delightful
> setting. No effort is too great when it comes to the choice of a colour.
> A pink can be aggressive or sweetish, pale, or like a tender blossom.
> Being in such a room can almost recall some of the loveliness felt
> under a fruit tree in bloom. *(1950/1991, p. 32)*

Far from being a random choice of colours, their usage is influenced by Goethe's colour theory in which he stated that particular colours create a 'special disposition'. Additionally, the method of application – whereby many thin washes of colour are applied, resulting in fine nuances reminiscent of these found in nature – is unique. The plant-based pigments cover a broad colour spectrum, which creates a sense of depth when applied in layers with gradual increments in the colour change.

7.3 A typical day, week and year

Every day, week and year in a Steiner kindergarten is organized according to a rhythmic pattern. The focus on rhythm is also seen in the specific activities such as verses, finger games and songs, as well as festivals and activities. For instance, each day is structured to incorporate periods of active free play, followed by quiet, concentrated phases. Furthermore, there is a rhythmic element running through the weekly and yearly activities. Despite this emphasis on rhythm, the intention is to provide a guiding force for the structure of the kindergarten day, rather than a strict, unadaptable, mechanistic time-frame.

7.3.1 Corner stones of the daily rhythm

As in all kindergartens, the day begins with children arriving, which in Waldorf-Steiner kindergartens typically begins with a period of 'free play'. As children come into the room they are individually greeted by a teacher or teachers. Attention is also given to the child's state as they arrive, and perhaps any particular objects they have brought with them (e.g. clothing, mood, concerns or perhaps a doll). These few moments of greeting are intended to help the child feel welcomed and comfortable in kindergarten. At this point the parent and teacher may also exchange any important or noteworthy information. The rest of the kindergarten day is then structured with alternating periods of free, self-directed play and whole-group activities.

The period of free play directly after arriving often helps a child to adjust back to the kindergarten surroundings, perhaps by playing with a favourite doll or building a tower. As the children play, the teachers are engaged in meaningful activities, be it preparing for the meal to come or mending a broken toy (Nicol and Taplin, 2012). Each child is free to play alone, with others, or perhaps simply watch or help a teacher preparing the meal. Some children may draw or weave, others build a fort or dress as princesses or knights, and still others sit quietly in a corner looking at a book. Although the teachers are available to answer questions or help resolve disagreements, or perhaps even to read or tell a story to a child who is struggling to get

into the day, they are careful to leave the children to play with as little adult interference or intrusion as possible. As the free play period draws to a close, a teacher will signal this by beginning to sing a tidying-up song and perhaps a gentle jingling of a bell. The children slowly finish their activities or games, and tidy up together with the teachers.

The next phase is then usually circle-time, when all the children and teachers gather together and sit in a circle, either on chairs or on the floor. The 20 or so minutes that follow are filled with a varied mix of songs, finger games and rhythmic activities, typically specific to the particular season or festival period.

After circle-time there is usually a 'washing-hands' song, and all children go together to the bathroom to wash hands ready for breakfast. They then return to the classroom to sit at the tables, which are laid and decorated to reflect the current season (for example, with spring flowers, or autumn leaves) and a candle in the centre. A grace is then said, and the candle is lit, before eating the meal. The meal is vegetarian and prepared with organic (or sometimes biodynamic) ingredients, and varies depending on the day of the week. Often it is grain-based, and a typical weekly rotation might comprise of rice pudding (Monday), barley rice (Tuesday), millet balls (Wednesday), homemade rye rolls (Thursday) and oat muesli and fruit (Friday). Generally, each meal would also be accompanied by freshly chopped fruit or vegetables.

Once the meal is finished and a short thank-you verse has been spoken, the next phase of outdoor play – come rain or shine! – begins. After dressing appropriately for the weather, children go out into the garden area, which is designed to maintain as much of its natural character as possible. Typically, there is little specialized play equipment, but many opportunities to hide, climb, run, balance, bake 'sand cakes' or help take care of the garden.

After around an hour (depending on the weather), the children start to become tired and hungry again, at which point everyone helps to tidy the garden before going inside for lunch. Children help to distribute food and perhaps with clearing dishes or washing up. In some kindergartens lunch is followed by a story or a puppet show; in others the story may take place before lunch, or perhaps during the circle-time earlier in the day.

Depending on the age of the children and the length of time they are in kindergarten, a quiet time or nap time may follow. Older children who do not require this period of rest may go back into the garden instead, or perhaps work on a craft activity. For children who remain in kindergarten for more of the day, they experience a similar pattern of activity to the morning – that is, periods of quieter, individual play followed by periods of more boisterous play, perhaps outside. Typically, there is a shared mid-afternoon snack, for example, of slices of fruit or vegetables.

7.3.2 Weekly and yearly rhythm

The weekly rhythm can be seen in the different emphasis and activities on each day of the week. For example, on one day of the week the children may do watercolour painting, on another handcrafting such as woodworking, and on yet another household tasks such as baking bread. Another day of the week may include crafting like sewing, or eurythmy[19] may be held once a week as well. In addition, some kindergartens also have a weekly rhythm running through their meals, such that a particular grain is prepared and eaten on a particular day of the week. As such, children may begin to recognize which day of the week it is by the meal being prepared – for example, it must be Monday because rice pudding is cooking.

The changing of the season is another clear rhythm in nature, and this too is experienced on a daily basis as children play in the garden. This natural rhythm of the year is further emphasized by a changing set of activities, festivals and rituals associated with each season. Many practical activities – such as harvesting fruit, collecting vegetation, building nests for hedgehogs, plaiting flower wreaths, making jam, crafting lanterns and tending to the flowerbeds – have a natural connection to particular times of the year. The teachers and children engage in these activities quite naturally in tune with the seasons. Each classroom also has a special seasonal display, often called the Nature Table, which changes to reflect the changing seasons. A small collection of items from nature – for example, flowers, fruit, nuts or pinecones – is brought inside and arranged with colourful cloths, a candle and perhaps

a picture or postcard as a reminder of the current season. Furthermore, the songs and stories heard change to reflect the changes during the year. There is also an emphasis on eating seasonally in Waldorf kindergartens (Kassner, 2011) – perhaps even produce harvested from the kindergarten's own garden.

Not only seasonal, cultural and religious festivals, but also the birthdays of the individual children are of great significance to the rhythm of the year. In addition, many Christian festivals – Easter, St Johns Day, Michaelmas, Harvest, Saint Martin's Day, Advent and Christmas – are celebrated. Depending on the individual constellation of a kindergarten, these celebrations may also be augmented or incorporated with festivals from other cultures, such as the Indian light festival of Divali or the Jewish festival of Hannukah. Regardless of which precise festivals are celebrated, their marking creates a secure orientation during the year, is associated with much anticipation, and influences the daily routine through the related preparations (e.g. crafting, decorating, baking....). A more extensive discussion of how festivals are celebrated in Waldorf-Steiner kindergartens, and the associated challenges, can be found in section 7.5.

Living into the cycle of the year can be a means to experience development and metamorphosis. For example, the grains sown at Easter time grow across the course of the spring and summer, until their harvest – like wheat in the late summer. In some kindergartens this wheat may actually be ground to make bread; in others, a few grains of wheat are gifted in a golden walnut at Christmas time, and these in turn are saved until the following Easter, at which point the cycle can begin again.

Other special ceremonies that mark particular celebrations include the preparation of a Christmas play in which all children take turns playing different characters in the weeks leading up to Christmas. Some kindergartens also hold an 'Advent Spiral' in which each child carries an unlit candle into the middle of the spiral to be lit from a central candle, and then places their candle at different points along the spiral until the whole spiral is filled with candles, emitting a gentle glow (see Prologue). Other highlights during the year include a summer festival – often timed to coincide with St John's Day – where children have the opportunity to jump over a fire (held by teachers!) and a farewell for the children leaving kindergarten for school Class 1.

One final important point to mention is that many of the festivals and activities that occur during the kindergarten year require a good deal of preparation to run smoothly. As such, there is some expectation that each family becomes involved with organizing festivals, handcraft evenings, educational talks, parent cafés, administrative and governance tasks, or kindergarten-community tasks.

These activities form an integral part of the shared educational experience and community building that characterize Waldorf education.

7.4 Transition to school

Preparation for the transition to school begins during the last kindergarten year in that children are given more responsibility – for example, in the form of special tasks (e.g. watering plants). In addition, they have the opportunity to take part in special, more challenging arts and crafts activities, such as weaving a doll-sized carpet or making a skipping rope from finger-crocheted rope and hand-made handles. These activities typically run across many months, and allow the children on the cusp of beginning school to carry out activities with less direct intervention from the teachers. These types of activities help to 'school' the skills necessary for formal education, such as staying task-focused, as well as fine and gross motor skills, in an enjoyable, playful way. Some kindergartens also organize special excursions, or have the children in their last year of kindergarten perform a puppet show for the younger children.

The culmination of the kindergarten year comes with the fare-welling of the children soon beginning school, in a ceremony in which they receive their special project work, and folders with their pictures and paintings from their time in kindergarten.

7.5 A look at international differences

Thankfully, in this age of homogeneity and commercialism, the world still hums and weaves – sometimes rising to tumult and chaos – with human and cultural diversity. As Steiner education has spread to the world, and the world has come to Steiner education institutions, it has encountered many different religions, cultures and traditions. In contrast to the beginnings of Steiner education in Central Europe, where probably four kinds of worldviews were likely dominant (i.e. Catholicism, Protestantism, Judaism and Atheism), kindergartens in the West and the East will likely have children from any range of backgrounds, adding, for example, Buddhism, Islam, Taoism, Hinduism and various indigenous cultures to the mix. A clear question arises: how should Steiner education relate to this diversity?

In answering this question, it is important to see that Steiner intended education (and anthroposophy) to be a cultural impulse, whose aim was not to stand above human culture, expounding abstractions from an ivory-tower pulpit. Instead, it is a pedagogical and humane impulse whose role is to help humankind to an ever-deeper understanding and appreciation of human culture. Perhaps it can be summed up as saying that it is far more important to be seeking for truth than to 'own' the truth. This attitude can fill the educator with reverence for the diversity in the world, respect for the freedom of others and, most importantly, a desire to live one's way into those around one. This makes Steiner education pedagogical, not evangelical, in nature, and equips her to meet the challenges of the future. The result of this fundamentally pedagogical attitude is that Steiner education can find a place in any ethnic community or culture, so long as willing parents and educators exist.

Steiner education may have begun in Germany, a country where the Christian festivals are traditionally celebrated, but the numerous schools and kindergartens that have sprouted up in every corner of the world are evidence enough that Steiner education need not be restricted to one particular culture. There are Steiner kindergartens in countries as diverse as Tibet, India, Australia, Egypt, Kenya, on American Indian reserves in the United States, in Brazilian Favelas, in Israeli Kibbutz and so on. The question may naturally arise as to how each of these different cultures interacts with Waldorf education and adapts it to their own environment, their own traditions and their own religions.

Interestingly, the founder of the Wolakota Waldorf kindergarten on the Sioux Native Indian reserve spoke of the many parallels he saw between Steiner education and his traditional Native Indian culture (Leber, 1997, p. 95). This alludes to the fact that the first step in adapting this education to a given culture is to find the parallels between that culture and Steiner education. For many traditional cultures, the qualities that form the foundation of Steiner education are also similarly important – for example, respect for children and nature. The spiritual conception implicit in Steiner education is also present in many traditional cultures, from Native Indian, to traditional African cultures, to Eastern religions such as Buddhism and Hinduism. As such, it is often a case of finding an external form that is appropriate for the culture in question. For example, whether a kindergarten chooses to celebrate Christian, Jewish, Muslim, Buddhist or Hindu festivals is not the critical point, but rather, the reverence and respect imbued through the celebration process itself.

This also fits with Steiner's nuanced and deep understanding of Christianity as a force for humankind, being far more than a mere religious doctrine. In numerous lectures, Steiner pointed out how the key teachings of Christianity were already present in, for example, Buddhism. Moreover, Christianity was preceded by other important religions, without which it could not have developed (e.g. Judaism, Buddhism, Zoroastrian). In this sense, Christianity is in other religions, and other religions are in her. From a theological viewpoint, one which Steiner also shared, the important point about Christianity was the sacrifice made by Christ, a God becoming flesh to be crucified by humankind. At the risk of simplification, this emphasizes more than anything the importance of deeds, not mere words and abstractions; deeds that are also needed in education, regardless of the prevailing culture and religion into which these deeds work.

Below are three portraits from teachers working in different Steiner kindergartens across the globe, from Nepal, South Africa and Israel. We selected these countries to provide an insight into how Steiner education is taken up in the most diverse of cultures, how festivals are celebrated, and how the education is adapted to meet the needs of the community it is serving.

7.5.1 Argaman Kindergarten in Israel
– a report from Noa Yemini

What is the significance of celebrating festivals? If we consider that children come from a spiritual world, it means that children in the first seven years of life are open and very connected to the experience of oneness with nature. If we look more broadly at the festivals – not so much from a religious perspective, but from a cultural perspective – we see that the festivals are also very connected to nature. Christmas, for example, and all the festivals around Christmas time, or Divali in India, are connected to nature – we can see this in different cultures, humankind overcoming darkness. In celebrating what is happening in nature, we are actually celebrating something pagan, a more universal experience of nature.

In celebrating Hannukah, for example, we also see this universal experience of the changing of light. The colours with which we choose to decorate the kindergarten room become more and more blue as we get towards Hannuka, and we create a more enclosed space. I like to fold paper stars and to hang them up, or make lanterns; and I also use less electric light, and light more candles at this time. The morning circle is also related to Hannuka. The stories we tell continue the theme – for example, we might tell the story of the firefly, the story of a star that forgot to shine. The moon told him not to go to earth, but in the end he came to earth and he turned into a firefly, and he had to remain on the Earth and couldn't go back to the stars…. All these things are leading up to Hannuka. Other traditions include baking doughnuts, and at festival time we celebrate with the children and their families, inviting each family to light a candle, which creates a small city of lights.

I think Waldorf-Steiner education is different to more mainstream education in a number of ways. In mainstream education we try to teach the child via his intellect, imagining him as a small adult, and in the process we forget that he has a different consciousness. He is always being prepared for something else, for something in the future, for Class 1, for Class 2, and so on. We forget that the child is sensitive and open to his environment.

What I try to do is let the child be, to live in the present. I don't prepare her for anything, because her development is a natural one, and rather, I try to provide her with everything she needs now, that she needs in the present, so that then she will be ready for the future. And what do children need? They need touch, warmth, love, adults in the environment who work physically, artistically and aesthetically, adults in the environment who know what they are doing, who can relate harmoniously to one another, and give children the feeling that the world is good and safe.

I experience a certain conflict between the materialistic, individualistic strivings of the modern world and the attempts to develop a more collective consciousness in the kindergarten setting. So how do we create this communal consciousness when it is no longer present in a natural form? It is often difficult to work against the external time pressures, too, and to allow children room to discover the world and the relations between different processes in their own time. In the eight years I have been teaching in kindergarten, I have also noticed that there are more and more children coming along with special needs. This has become the norm – children who are very sensitive and require more individual attention. How do we create a cohesive kindergarten group whilst still attending to all the individual needs and individualities of the various children? Another frustration I experience is a lack of cooperation and understanding from parents.

Although our kindergartens are officially recognized and there is a degree of external monitoring from the council and government, we only receive a small amount of funding, and as such are not beholden to the officials. There are certain regulations which are not always compatible with Steiner principles and can create challenges, such as not being allowed to light candles, or not being permitted to use hand towels in the bathroom. Additionally, we are expected to meet certain educational goals, such as teaching counting. In order to meet these requirements, we try to engage the children in a practical task, such as counting chairs for a specific purpose, and we avoid intellectual activities as much as possible.

It is my belief that children today need to have more experience with nature. They need to go into the forest as much as possible, for example, and to interact with the natural world, with water, air and earth. This world of natural forms is in stark contrast to the world where children spend much of their time – the world of buildings, of rules, of electricity. For this reason, in our kindergarten we try to have objects in their natural state, and allow children to engage with real materials. Also, it is important for children to experience whole processes – for example, planting calendula seeds, watching them grow, harvesting the flowers, drying them, and then making soap from the dried flowers. Similarly, the process of baking bread allows children to observe every step, and to develop a deeper understanding of the interconnectedness of life. I also believe that the rhythms of the day, week, month and year, in which children move from states of free play to more directed activities, all in an aesthetically pleasing environment, are important aspects of the Waldorf-Steiner kindergarten experience.

7.5.2 Tashi Waldorf School Kindergarten, Kathmandu, Nepal – a report from Chandra Kumari Tamang

Currently, I serve as a kindergarten teacher at Tashi Waldorf School. I have been part of the Waldorf-Steiner movement for the last 21 years, when it was first introduced to me by an Israeli lady named Meyrov Mor. Initially, I was unfamiliar with the Waldorf-Steiner movement, but as I continued to work at Bal Mandir Waldorf Kindergarten, I started to develop an in-depth knowledge about the approach. As a part of teacher training I received a golden opportunity to participate in the three-year training at Emerson College, England. The training helped me to know more about anthroposophy, ways of running a kindergarten within a local culture, a deeper understanding of early childhood development, and a lot of artistic work. After receiving training, I returned and started to teach at Tashi Waldorf School as a kindergarten teacher.

So far, the government of Nepal hasn't exerted any pressure on Tashi Waldorf School. However, despite educating parents about Waldorf-Steiner education during the admission process, our parents frequently complain that their children learn later in the Waldorf School as compared to private and public schools. They want Waldorf education to start their children's reading and writing at an earlier age. The high turnover of students is in part related to the lack of reading and writing in earlier years.

A large percentage of our parents come from a poor economic background with little or no education. Parents fear that if they continue with their children's education at the school, then their children won't be able to compete with other children of their age. So, it's a challenging task for the school and teachers to make parents fully appreciate the values of Waldorf education. To counteract this problem we conduct parents' meetings four times a year where we give information about Waldorf education and its values. Parents are slowly realising its benefits for their children's future, and some of them have started attending various Waldorf-Steiner training courses that are being held in Nepal.

Tashi Waldorf School has students from various cultural backgrounds, particularly Hindus and Buddhists – so we celebrate major Hindu and Buddhist festivals. Amongst major Hindu festivals, we celebrate 'Tihar', which is also regarded as a festival of lights where candles and Diyo are lit at home.

Tihar is a five-day long Hindu festival celebrated in Nepal in late October or in early November during the harvest moon season. It is second only to 'Dashain' as the most important Hindu festival observed in Nepal. It is considered to be of great importance, as it makes a contribution not only to humans and to the gods, but also to the animals, like the crows, cows and dogs that maintain an intimate relationship with human beings. Tihar represents the divine attachment between humans and other animals.

Preparation for Tihar celebrations begins a month before the festival. Kindergarten teachers get ready for the Tihar celebration by performing the following steps:

1. Harvest the rice in the school's field
2. Pick marigolds from the garden with the children, in order to create a garland
3. Gather leaves on a nature walk with the children, for making a candle spiral
4. Papier-mâché kindergarten windows in seven Tika colours – white, purple, orange, blue, red, green and golden-yellow
5. Clean kindergartens and playhouse with the children in preparation for Goddess Laxmi's visit
6. Prepare the nature table – draping is gold, red and yellow. On the table there is a figure or painting of Laxmi. The table is decorated with paper chains, candle, incense, a Puja (prayer) bell and a Tika plate
7. Make candle holders out of apples

Craft activities with the children:

1. Make coloured paper chains to decorate the Puja table
2. Make candles for the children to take home
3. Grind rice into flour to make 'Sel Roti' (Tihar donuts)
4. Make marigold garlands to decorate the playhouse

Celebration on the day:

1. The children have free play in the morning
2. Toilet, washing hands and morning snack
3. Telling a story
4. Performing prayers and rituals
5. Offer Tika and Prasad
6. Candle and Diyo (a kind of lantern made of mud) lighting
7. Decorate the playhouse and singing in the garden
8. Lunch
9. Nap-time
10. Toilet and go home

Festival Lunch Menu:

1. Sel roti made of rice flour
2. Razma – bean curry
3. Aloo char – potato pickle

To date we haven't celebrated Christian festivals: rather, we adopt festivals from our local culture.

Waldorf-Steiner education is a major need of today's world. Though it seems to some people that this education is suitable only for Christians, as it originated from Europe, I think this education is appropriate for all religions – viz. Hindus, Buddhists, Muslims, etc. – if it is adapted to local tradition and culture.

Waldorf-Steiner education has become a global education. Today, most of the parents are obsessed with seeing their children become doctors, engineers or pilots, but very few are thinking of helping their children to be a good human being. Technology has dominated the twenty-first century, with ever-more work being automated, thus requiring less human labour. If we let robots do all the work, I fear for children's futures. I hear people from outside Waldorf education complain that we use quite old-fashioned methods to teach the children. They maintain that by prohibiting younger children from using technology, Waldorf-Steiner education hasn't taken account of current-day needs. To some extent they have a point, but it's not good to let children use computers, mobile phones and ipads under the pretext that 'we're in the Digital Age'. I think we should care about and pay attention to child development. I cannot imagine what the future holds if we let children use technology, eat junk food, use antibiotic medicines, play with plastic toys and if we give them synthetic clothes to wear.

The world is changing at such an alarming pace that it's beyond our comprehension. When I look back at my childhood I clearly remember going to school at the age of six. Before going to school, I used to imitate my parents' behaviours like cooking food, washing clothes, doing the dishes, cleaning the house, stitching worn-out clothes, fetching water, farming, and so on. To me, these activities used to be like play rather than work. I used to have a lot of fun doing all these activities, and it used to be a good example for us to learn from them and to imitate.

Similarly, I used to live in a joint family rather than a nuclear family. Today, it's like a dream, especially for children living in cities, to witness and learn these activities. These children don't know where the food they eat comes from. As everything is bought in shops, they think that things are produced in the shop itself. Also, children are unable to imitate their parents' work, as they're now not able to see real work. Parents are at work all day, whereas children watch television and play on computers, mobiles or on the internet. Children are deprived of real feelings, real work, and speaking and listening to people. Many parents in cities feel proud when their children stay at home all day watching television, playing computer games, using mobiles etc. But they are totally unaware of what the future holds for their children who are used to such daily lives.

In summary, I think that Waldorf-Steiner education helps the development of children in a natural way in a natural environment, including many aspects like eurythmy, biodynamics and visual art. It helps to heal children, and should be spread all over the world so that every child has the opportunity to experience it.

7.5.3 Imhoff Waldorf School kindergarten, Cape Town, South Africa – a report from Joy Levin

Three communities feed into Imhoff Waldorf. The first, Ocean View, is more established, with proper houses that are about 30 years old. Secondly, there is Masiphumelele, the informal black township – a lively community mixing the predominant Xhosa population, but also nationals from other African countries. Finally, there is Redhill, which is more rural and quite isolated, but safer. The school attempts a very lively sponsorship programme, bringing children from all three of these communities as well as the wealthier areas around. Sponsorship includes arranging transport, providing remedial education, and making sure that the community is included in all parent meetings, events, camps and festivals.

I have been a kindergarten teacher there for 12 years. We only got solar-energy electricity five years ago, and it is still mostly candle light and sunshine! Each class is a little wooden prefabricated house, and the gardens are full of indigenous trees and bushes. The school is located on a farm, and there are camels and goats, predatory birds and porcupines. The school has a very strong sense of nature.

The celebration of festivals is a considerable part of being a Waldorf teacher and of building community. Residing in an African society and the southern hemisphere influencing the seasons both come into play when designing a festival. I once listened to an anthroposophical priest speak about the southern hemisphere. One can think of it only according to the seasons, and then it would make sense to have Christmas in July, and St Johns in mid-summer December. But as Richard Goodhall said, it is a cosmic festival, and is not only about the seasons: in some ways we are living in the shadow of the experience.

Take autumn, which for us is Easter. We are the autumn of the spring. How does that manifest? In Cape Town particularly, winter brings rain, so in some ways that does create growth in terms of the plants which struggle in the dry heat of the summer. Harvest has its relationships to bunnies and chickens, and stories like 'The Little Red Hen' can show the compassion of sharing, and the opposite in selfishness; and in the end, they share the bread.

One of our first teachers, Estelle Bryer, wrote beautiful material for Christmas and Easter. Her puppet show managed to bring together the resurrection theme with gardening of harvest time. It is a story of a bunny who lives in a very dry, dead garden, and who becomes increasingly weak. A gnome finds the bunny and takes it to Mother Earth, who offers him a garden where there is enough rain and sun and wind. The bunny loves his new home, and becomes strong. A hen is sitting on her nest and asks the bunny to watch her eggs for an afternoon while she goes and looks for food. The bunny, happy to have new friends, agrees and sits on the eggs. In that time, a black crow comes and tries to steal the eggs and attacks the bunny. Again, the bunny is nearly killed, but does manage to protect the eggs. Then an angel comes and blesses the bunny for the protection he has provided, and he comes alive again. I have done this puppet show many times, and always enjoy the magic of it. This story also relates to a flourishing garden, which the children craft themselves. Little eggs are found in their individual gardens, sometimes with a hand-made gnome and bunny.

Sometimes if Easter falls later in the year, then I will focus just on the harvest. I have made apple bags and sung horse and apple songs. We have used 'The Three Little Pigs' and done apple bobbing at the fair. Horse reins, felt baskets and eggs are other harvest crafts. It is for the teacher to decide whether they are focusing on harvest, or Easter, or both. I have had a fire and cooked potatoes, and Easter egg hunts are always a great excitement.

Our St Johns ends up being the mid-winter festival. The Easter and spring festivals are celebrated with the children only, and the winter festival and Christmas are conducted with the parents. The mid-winter festival is really one of the most beautiful and enchanting, as well as being community building. In the kindergarten, we make lanterns and tell a story of how the lantern becomes a home to Father Sun, as the sun starts to become less each day. At the festival, we either do a ring about gnomes in the winter bringing seeds to Mother Earth and calling all the gnomes to celebrate the festival of St John. Otherwise I have done puppet shows like 'The Little Girl and the Lantern', as well as the play of 'The Seven Ravens'. Afterwards, bags of sand and candles are laid on a pathway and the teacher and children, followed by the parents, follow the lit pathway with their lanterns, singing the songs. Everyone comes to gather at the fire and we sing together, then eat soup and drink hot chocolate. Having nearly no electricity, everything is candle-lit and dark, and the magic this festival brings is so delightful. It really encapsulates the inner light of the dark night, as we walk through the lit garden under the fresh night sky. It is often cold, nearly raining, and there is a strong connection to the weather. In this way, St Johns makes sense as a candle-lit experience, along with the bigger fire.

In the primary school, there is one large bonfire, which the Grade 7s light. The fire becomes a mid-winter experience.

Christmas, on the other hand, is during the already-hot summer. The original Christmas stories make sense, as we have more of a Middle Eastern climate, rather than snow and sleighs. Spring is a very interesting one to work out, in terms of the typical St Michael picture of autumn and the sword of discernment through the darkness of the dragon's dens. For us, it is spring. How does that work? What I have found is that children naturally begin to play dragons at this time, and act with a real spring in their temperament. The dragons also come up when the rains have wetted the ground and everything is growing. In this case, it is the discernment amongst all the growth, as opposed to in a dark tunnel. That is, it is discerning when there is too much, and finding what is golden and relevant.

We love woodwork in the spring, making swords and sanding them. Children love sewing crowns and frog ponds and finishing their weaving bags. I also love making sword sheaths. Golden cloaks dyed with turmeric, and anything to do with flowers. The sleeping beauty story brings the spring picture, which also includes the darkness within the colours of the twelve fairies. 'Snowflake and the Dragon' is a favourite, despite having much more northern hemisphere images for the months. Spring, Michael and dragons seem to have found their harmony together.

Another great festival activity we do in spring is to make butter, which then goes with the dragon bread. The butter-making is accompanied by a story of a little mouse who falls into the cream and remembers his mother's words to 'never give up, always persist'. And as he does this in the cream, it turns to butter.

I feel that mainstream schooling no longer understands play, or children. I worked for a term in the rural Transkei homelands, at a little Waldorf school in a hut. My assistant had only worked at a Christian school, where the three year-olds were forced to sit at their desk, learn to write their name and colour in. At first she was terrified of play, and she was convinced that the children wouldn't like it, either. Afterwards I realised that she was afraid it would turn to chaos; but within three weeks she was amazed that the children had found a balance within themselves, the chores and the play.

The main difference in the Waldorf-Steiner approach is very considerable: first that they allow time to play, and for the children to find their own sense of regulation as a group, which is guided but not controlled by the teacher. The understanding that rhythm is the most important thing for the young child, and having a breathing in and out, enable the deep physical development of the young child, along with their imagination. Story-telling is the way to engage the children's interest and empathy, and to create a social connection between the individual children as a group. Crafts and artistic expression allow for individual will development, as well as emergent skills. And story-telling and movement become the teacher's main input. This is so different from the segmented, over-focused scheduling of public education, which has no materials or time for real play.

In terms of bringing the African dimension into the work, I think it starts with the children in the class – who they are, and what they bring. The different languages bring opportunities during ring-time and stories. Observing nature and the nature stories are usually about what is truly around us. There are lovely African fairy tales, such as the Zulu tale and 'The Winning of Kwelenga'. There are beautiful blessings and songs. Having assistants from the local cultures in the class is such an opportunity. Two of the lead teachers at Imhoff are Xhosa. My own assistant for the last three years was Zimbabwean, speaking Shona. Having two teachers brings different natures, skills and languages.

7.6 Relation to other preschool traditions

In terms of many of the specific activities that one can expect to encounter in a Waldorf-Steiner kindergarten, there is much overlap with other educational approaches. Indeed, much of the Steiner content has been gathered together out of other traditions and fields of life: this is only right and proper, because a constructive educational impulse needs to work with what is available, building upon the latter. In this way it remains connected to, and not aloof from, contemporary culture. However, this conscious adopting and developing from other approaches is done out of the comprehensive understanding of the human being outlined in this book. Other educational approaches are also built around views of the human being, although few of these are as novel and comprehensive as those insights formulated by Steiner. Finally, of course, there is much to be learned and gained from looking into other approaches and philosophies.

7.6.1 Montessori

Every Steiner teacher has probably one experience in common: they have been mistaken, probably many times, for a Montessori educator! Indeed, Montessori and Steiner seem to have become synonyms for the expression of 'some kind of non-mainstream education system'. In reality, however, and contrary to these casual lay conceptions, the approaches are fundamentally different, although not without some commonalities.

As with Steiner education, Montessori education also began as a social impulse. Maria Montessori (1870–1952) was Italy's first female medical graduate, but she soon began to notice that a new educational approach was needed (Kley-Auerswald and Schmutzler, 2015). She founded the *Casa dei Bambini* in a poor quarter of Rome, thus joining the ranks of important Central European educational reformers – Friedrich Fröbel, Johann Pestallozi, Johann Herbart and Johann Comenius. Her movement quickly spread, such that from the first school in 1907 there were more than 100 by 1916.

Again, similar to Steiner, Montessori believed that children passed through stages of development, and her philosophy was also a spiritual one. Children are seen as learning from life, learning with all the senses; and alongside intellectual development, emotional and spiritual development are important. In Montessori kindergartens, the materials are also generally made of natural materials. As in Steiner education, the overarching approach is also centred around supporting self-initiative (e.g. 'Help me to do it by myself').

However, if one actually stands in a Steiner and in a Montessori educational setting, one quickly notices a large number of differences. First, the aesthetics offer a different experience. Whereas in Steiner education, care is taken to soften the surroundings by draping silks, and rounding out corners to create an imaginative and protected environment (see section 7.2), Montessori kindergartens seem a little more practically arranged. Shelves filled with wooden toys are present, as are little corners or huts into which children can retreat. However, a philosophical difference immediately becomes apparent: in Montessori the toys are generally designed to convey something directly conceptual to the children. For instance, some toys are designed to facilitate the learning of mathematical concepts, while others convey physical laws (Kley-Auerswald, 2017). In contrast, Steiner toys are often asymmetrical and more natural looking, again (as described earlier) because the idea is to allow children to remain in an imaginative world for longer.

This difference in the room set-up and the toys is based on a fundamental philosophical difference. In Montessori education, children are expected to teach themselves, with kindergarten teachers acting as facilitators of this learning. Montessori herself was against the likes of imaginative play, believing that, for example, a child should be redirected from riding on a broom as if it were a horse. Instead, for Montessori a child needs to learn that a broom is for sweeping (Lillard, 2013).[20]

Montessori education also takes the individuality of the child very seriously, thus tailoring education to individuals, attempting to recognize latent talents and interests, and help the children unfold them. This leads to a different approach to academic learning. In Montessori settings, if a child shows interest in reading at age two, for example, then the teacher helps the child learn to read at this age. Consequently, Montessori children learn to read earlier than other children, although this advantage disappears after several years (Lillard and Else-Quest, 2006). In contrast, in Steiner education, one would tend to view a child's interest in reading as arising from imitation, and would react, not by forbidding the child to read or write, but by ensuring that there were other options available that place less strain on early intellectual forces.

In short, some overlap between Montessori and Steiner is present, but marked differences exist in both the underlying philosophy and in the details in which these are practised.

7.6.2 Emmi Pikler

Another doctor who has had a considerable influence on education, and an increasing one on Steiner education, is the Hungarian Emmi Pikler (1907–1978). Pikler developed insights, in particular into the first years of life, in her work with poor Hungarian children. Her educational considerations are proving fruitful for Steiner education, as this begins to extend downward into the first three years of post-partum life. Pikler had a keen sense of observation, and noticed that communication with very young children was more than possible. She also described infant motor development in great detail. The four pillars of her education are an attentive and dignified relationship to small children; the facilitation of autonomous motor development; an emphasis on free play; and an appropriate shaping of the physical environment (Ostermayer, 2013). There is much in both Steiner and Pickler education that is built around this careful, mindful observation of, and interaction with, small children.

7.6.3 Forest kindergartens

A new approach goes back to the roots of the word kindergarten (meaning 'garden of children') by running these in woodland settings (Miklitz, 2016). In forest kindergartens, children spend most of their time outdoors, regardless of the season. In and of itself, forest kindergartens do not represent a new educational philosophy, but instead differ mostly via the new physical setting. Being located in forests, there are of course many unique features and educational adjustments that are necessary to ensure a safe and prosperous atmosphere. The clear nature experiences that children at this age can gather, along with sensory and motor experiences, are surely enriching. Studies show that such surroundings work positively on children's social behaviour and attention (Taylor et al., 2001).

Although Steiner education would typically balance nature experience with indoors time, there is a clear appeal of forest kindergartens, particularly in a modern society which tends to be removed from nature.

7.6.4 State kindergartens

Moving beyond these alternative approaches, it is also insightful to compare Steiner education to mainstream approaches. Of course, the danger here is that mainstream is a broad term extending across many different countries and cultures, so our selected focus is of necessity simplified. Just think how varied different children's experiences attending different kindergarten within the same city can be!

However, as addressed earlier (sections 6.2 and 6.3), key differences between state and Steiner approaches tend to exist in terms of the kind of learning offered, expectations, and how such learning 'standards' are defined, monitored and enforced. Steiner education generally views early educational standards with some scepticism, as these often lead to 'stress, surveillance and modernity', as House (2000) describes it. Nevertheless, there is also much overlap in what milestones and goals the standards set, and what children in a Steiner kindergarten meet (Nicol, 2015).

Most crucially, it is important to recognize that no kindergarten or early-years institution writes their leitbild philosophy and approach in a manner that betrays something untoward! Often these are replete with benevolent or complex-sounding terms and educational jargon, expressed in a form that one could hardly disagree with (e.g. creative, developmentally appropriate, social, self-directed). As a result, there is often a convergence in such terminology across most kindergarten philosophies, just as there is a strong convergence in the time-consuming daily-care activities required in all institutions working with small children. The educator has to either transform these daily-care activities into important educational moments, as advocated by Pikler in particular, and also fill daily activities with an appropriate mood. This is what good teachers do, regardless of the institution.

Indeed, it is not impossible to find mainstream kindergartens in Germany and northern Europe that again share many of the external features of Steiner education. For example, festivals are celebrated; time is spent outdoors; free play is seen as important; and movement, music, sensory experiences and artistic activities may also be emphasized. Despite these external similarities, there can still be quite appreciable differences, too, in the combination of what is offered, how these are carried out, and the view that the teachers have of the children.

A second distinguishing feature is also found in the aesthetics, including the feel of the room and the institution in general (see section 7.2). For example, state kindergartens tend to be decorated using brighter colours, and are generally 'busier' and less restful. Similarly, the diet that children are offered (section 6.5), and in particular how much the educators are present and authentic in their interactions with the children (6.7), may differ.

Further differences depend on the institution and what is currently fashionable. Susceptibility to adopting the latest educational fashions or policy is all the more likely if a comprehensive view of the human being is not anchored in both the educational philosophy and constant self-education of the teachers. Thus, many kindergartens the world over include packaged phonics and language-support programmes based on a questionable evidential basis (see section 8.2), whereas in Steiner settings more natural and imaginative means are preferred (see 6.3.3).

An increasing number of kindergartens is avidly adopting electronic media (see 8.3). Others have integrated democratic principles, regulating that children need to be able to vote in determining what is on offer, which can counter natural imitation impulses as well as over-awe the children. Interestingly, such an approach is common in Reggio Emilia kindergartens, which have their roots in communal management and communist principles (Lingenauber, 2011). Although the need for sensory experiences and movement may also be recognized, in state institutions this is often mandated to be monitored by evaluations and learning assessment.

Another distinguishing feature is found in the role of the teacher (see also section 6.6). In Steiner education, the teacher generally works in the background, trying not to interfere unnecessarily in children's inner worlds, and certainly not intruding into play to impart numeracy skills or explain the definitional meanings of words. For example, we have observed how, in state settings, a teacher will embed him- or herself into a child's activity, such as playing with objects, and exhort the children to count the objects out loud. From time to time, a Steiner teacher might direct children to certain activities as well; however, more typically a teacher would engage in something that a child might find inviting and wish to join in out of his or her own impetus (e.g. grinding wheat, repairing toys). A Steiner teacher also takes a more subtle approach to language support, not imposing this but instead, perhaps choosing words carefully, paying heed to how they are articulated, and focusing on imparting rich language via songs and stories.

Another difference is typically seen in the concept of the child's will (see section 3.4). Whereas the Steiner teacher focuses on educating with and through the will (e.g. via imitation), the state teacher often focuses on directly shaping behaviour and teaching thoughts (e.g. 'Be nice to each other'). This will-concept leads to a more child-centred and flexible approach to education, as opposed to a mechanical adherence to rules.

7.6.5 Scandinavian education: Longing for the Northern lights

Much of the world looks towards Scandinavia as a role model, with its child-centred, play-based kindergartens symbolizing a paradisiacal state compared to the standards-driven, pressurized assessment culture found in kindergartens elsewhere. Moreover, the top performance of Scandinavian countries in PISA studies has fuelled the impassioned flames saying that Scandinavian approaches lead to better achievement.

Interestingly, others have pointed out that in the case of the former first-placed PISA country Finland, she achieved in the top echelon due to the structured education system that was in place before educational reforms in the early 1990s. The long-term result of these liberal and child-centred reforms is argued by some to have actually reduced achievement – hence Finland is now sliding down the rankings.

In terms of external features, there is much to admire and applaud in Scandinavian early care centres. In comparison to those in England, for example, in Sweden there are no formal standards and academic content was (until recently) largely absent, and it is generally not directly taught (Pramling, 2004). Children spend time outside, regardless of the weather, with a focus on social and motor skills, as opposed to reading and numeracy. Moreover, the nutrition is generally healthy, home-made and low sugar.

Despite these many positive sides, there are still aspects of these kindergartens that create a different overall feel compared to Steiner kindergartens. Beginning with the aesthetics, institutions – depending on one's taste – typically appear starker and less homely looking than Steiner settings, which is often also reflected in the play materials. Interestingly, Swedish and other northern European kindergartens follow a strong democratic process (called 'participation'), meaning that children are involved in many decisions (Pramling, 2004). In Steiner kindergartens, the attempt is made to not overwhelm children by offering too many choices, following the Plato maxim whereby 'excessive freedom leads to excessive slavery' (see section 5.2.1).

Finally, again because the view of the human being is so different, Swedish kindergartens have allowed the year preceding school entry to be swallowed up by preparing children for school. This foot-in-the-door approach to intellectualizing early childhood is guarded against in Steiner education (see section 8.1). Also, it is not uncommon for phonics and reading to be taught in Nordic kindergartens, albeit purportedly in a more child-friendly way. Moreover, Sweden has moved over to a highly centralized early-years curriculum with educational goals and standards (Pramling, 2004).

Turning to Denmark, which in contrast to Sweden has a highly decentralized curriculum and is also rated as having a very high educational quality, differences to Steiner are also clear. Denmark's relatively hands-off curriculum still formulates five educational goals, which from a Steiner perspective seem quite abstract (Jensen and Langsted, 2004). Goals include the democratic principle whereby children help determine what is on offer, and giving children an 'understanding of cultural values' (our emphasis). Pressure is increasing for Denmark to introduce a highly centralized plan, and it will be interesting to see whether this can be kept at bay. Of course, there are many similarities between the Danish and Steiner systems, such as a child-centred focus and the absence of academic instruction (ibid.).

In short, the devil really is in the detail, and the detail – when consciously created – arises out of the mood created by the educators' commitment to constantly deepening their knowledge and understanding of children.

7.7 Beyond the kindergarten stage...?

Traditionally, children attend Steiner kindergartens until they are around seven years old. This is becoming increasingly more difficult in the modern Western education system, however, where formal school education sometimes starts as early as age four (see section 8.2). Nonetheless, solutions to this problem are often found, and it remains the case that many children who have attended Steiner kindergartens first enter formal (Steiner) education at age 6 or 7.

There are a number of striking differences about the format of a Steiner school, when compared with many other education systems. First, children typically remain in the same class, with the same class teacher, for the first eight years of school. This allows a secure relationship to develop between the teacher and students, the teacher to develop a deeper understanding of the personalities and needs of the children, and a strong class community to take shape.

Secondly, the structure of the day follows a familiar pattern, with around the first 90 minutes of each day being devoted to the main lesson, be that reading, writing, form drawing (Kutzli, 2007) or mathematics (broadening to include subjects such as history, chemistry or biology in the upper classes). The rest of the day is comprised of lessons in a variety of areas, including handcrafts, eurythmy, foreign languages, music, sport and perhaps religion.

Thirdly, the main subjects of reading/writing, mathematics and form drawing are taught in blocks or epochs. This means that during the main lesson for a period of 3–6 weeks, only one of these subjects is taught. Each of the main subjects is taught intensively for a period of time, before cycling around to another subject, allowing an intensive focus on one area before letting it rest and ripen for a period of time, and then revisiting and extending that subject in the next block.

In stark contrast to the strong academic push in most state curricula, the focus during the first one to two years of the Steiner school lies heavily on the development of language and the aesthetic. The letters of the alphabet, for example, are introduced by way of story, in which each letter is embedded. Out of the story emerges the form of each letter, which the children themselves then draw. In this way, children are introduced to the letters first through their own handwriting, and reading evolves out of the process of writing (Allanson and Teensma, 2018). Much emphasis is placed on oral communication in the first two school years, with many fairy tales being told, songs sung, and rhymes and verses learnt.

Another important feature of the Waldorf school curriculum includes a particular appreciation of the stage of childhood that a class is in (see section 5.2). That is, the structure of the curriculum is developed to reflect the changing nature of children. For example, Nordic mythology is taught during the fourth class, as children are typically quite temperamental in this phase, much like the Nordic gods themselves. In the sixth and seventh classes, when children are hitting puberty and may question their place in the world, the history lessons relate to the Romans and the Middle Ages in preparation for the Enlightenment. As much as possible, each subject area flows through into others – for example, history into religion, the natural sciences flow into art – as Steiner saw premature specialization as an unhealthy influence on childhood (Steiner (1919/2000).

As discussed earlier, imitation is a potent force during the first seven years of life (section 6.1.1), and imitation is intimately connected with the will. In contrast, Steiner believed that the second seven years of life are characterized by a strong connection with the feeling life, and as such, education in this phase should occur with this in mind. Practically speaking, a solid relationship between a teacher and a student is crucially important, hence the importance of a secure classroom environment. Learning through music and the arts, as well as via rhythm and repetition (in the form of verses and rhymes, often learnt by heart) are also appropriate in this phase.

Lastly, the latter phase of schooling, after age 14, can be characterized as education via the thinking or education in autonomy (i.e. freehood). At this point, more independent, analytical work can be expected from students, and material that was taught during the earlier years of school is often revisited in a more conscious manner. This is in stark contrast with many current state curricula, where children just entering school are expected to 'critically analyse texts'. From a Steiner perspective, it is desirable for children to first observe phenomena from many points of view before coming to a judgement, and such critical thinking is more natural and appropriate for children from adolescence onwards.

In a Nutshell

- The historical development of Steiner-Waldorf and its international practice provide further insights into educational principles.

- The environment can be employed as a 'third teacher'.

- Cornerstones of the daily, weekly and yearly rhythms provide coherency and aesthetic/cultural value.

- Insight into international kindergarten settings from Israel, Nepal and South Africa provide insight into how the approach can be implemented in diverse cultures.

- Comparisons with state, Scandinavian, Montessori and Pikler approaches reveal many commonalties and differences.

CHAPTER 8

Challenges to and for Steiner Education

> Waldorf students – who have probably been treated more as individuals than is usually the case – have to be sent out into life; otherwise, having a Waldorf school makes no sense at all. Students must not become estranged from contemporary life to the extent that they can only criticize what they meet outside.
>
> *(Steiner, 1921–1922/2003, p. 126)*

Steiner education constitutes one of the largest independent kindergarten and school movements in the world. Undoubtedly, this has enriched the educational landscape and the lives of many people. However, due to its growing popularity Steiner education increasingly features in the public eye, occasionally in a less-than-positive light. Perhaps as a result of certain elements of the philosophy, which are sometimes misunderstood or misrepresented, the educational approach can raise eyebrows, or is even met with open scorn and derision. This presents a number of challenges, both real and due to misconception, to which we turn in this chapter.

If one takes an honest look at the history and practice of Steiner education, there are clearly recognizable instances in which suggestions and myths have become firmly established 'dogmas' without sufficient differentiation and contextualization. Historical examples here have included an overly rigid adherence to daily rhythms or types of acceptable interactions with children, a rejection of popular culture (e.g. football), or excluding families that own a television. Taking one of these examples, although there may well be good reasons to limit television usage (see section 8.3), a truly open educational approach has to work pedagogically with the children who arrive at its doors.

Indeed, challenges are aplenty! Many families interested in Steiner schools may have difficulty, in some form or other, with the spiritual aspects of this approach, which we speak to in section 8.1, below. In many countries, there is strong external pressure to increase the academic focus of Steiner education, this we address in 8.2. A further challenge arises through the spread of electronic media (see section 8.3); and finally we turn to challenges facing the deepening of the Steiner education approach (8.4).

8.1 Spirituality, religion and anthroposophy

> Please understand that a Waldorf school – or any school that might spring from the anthroposophic movement – would never wish to teach anthroposophy as it exists today. I would consider this the worst thing we could do. Anthroposophy in its present form is a subject for adults and, as you can see from the color of their hair, often quite mature adults.
>
> *(Steiner, 1921–1922/2003, p. 122)*

As the above quotation makes clear, Steiner believed that anthroposophy was something that should be used to deepen and sharpen the teacher's perception and understanding of life, but that it should not be taught or explained in school. Needless to say, teaching anthroposophy to kindergarten children would be more absurd still, aside from being nigh on impossible to actually do. For some, however, the very fact that a verse might be said, or a festival celebrated in which a word such as 'God' might be mentioned, is reason enough to raise arms against the very existence of Steiner education. As such, a cursory internet search reveals a number of websites dedicated to warning parents about the dangers of Steiner education. So let us examine these perceived dangers more closely.

Turning to the first criticism that children attending Steiner kindergartens are being somehow indoctrinated, it is difficult to see what basis underpins this claim. Most of the time is spent in free play, crafting, listening to stories, preparing meals or going for walks. Perhaps it could be argued that celebrating the Christian festivals in European countries is indoctrination; but if so, then accusing Steiner education of indoctrination is more or less equivalent to accusing society of indoctrination, because public holidays are legislated for Christmas and Easter. Perhaps then saying a verse or grace before meals, or as part of a festival, is a form of indoctrination? From an educational point of view, saying a verse before a meal brings rest into the room, creating an aesthetically pleasing meal atmosphere. It also teaches children manners and virtues, such as waiting for others, learning to put the service of bodily needs after higher aesthetic principles, such as gratitude to nature and humankind for providing the meal.

Celebrating festivals – in the case of Europe, the Christian festivals – is also seen by some as antiquated, 'religious' or eurocentric. As previously mentioned, festivals need not necessarily be Christian, but are typically reflective of the community of children attending the kindergarten (see section 7.5). Festivals, be they Christian or otherwise, bring a structure and beauty into kindergarten life. Children enjoy preparing for them and they anticipate the various activities.

Moreover, each festival is phenomenologically symbolic for important events in nature – through celebrating these, children learn to feel and perceive subtle forces working into the year. Christmas – the birth of light into pure darkness! Easter – the birth of life into dead nature! May day, relishing in the delights of spring, a lightness and gaiety that sweeps one into the summer. St John's – the beginning of summer, fire and heat being poured through nature. Harvest festivals to connect children with the seasonality of produce and nature. Michaelmas is a festival of courage – the courage needed to plunge into the descending darkness, heralding the light to arrive in the depths of winter. Chanukah, Divali, Tihar, Chinese New Year, Spring Festivals – these all have a deep significance that can be integrated well into kindergarten life. Celebrated in this light, such festivals have nothing to do with religious dogma but instead, provide a beauty, structure and gratitude to and for life. Of course, educators need to find a way to celebrate the festivals that is appropriate to the children in their care, and in the culture and hemisphere in which they live (see section 7.3.2).

For some, Steiner schools have the feeling of being 'a bit closed off' from the outside world. Sometimes, perhaps, teachers and parents of kindergartens and schools respond dogmatically, or in a superior tone to questions and suggestions from the outside. Perhaps, seeking refuge in a Steiner school from a difficult and hostile outside world is a modus that some adopt. Further, as mentioned earlier, when one believes that one is on the path of self-development, one can fall prey to the most cruel and unpleasant self-delusions. Indeed, there is a very real danger that alternative education systems become a clique. Teachers and parents must guard steadfastly against this possibility, and as described earlier, this can be done through hard and practical work, greeting as much as possible that which comes towards one with openness, reserving judgement at times, and being a student of life. Back in the 1920s, Steiner saw such dangers becoming reality. He constantly said that teachers need to take an interest in life and work productively orientated towards society. Moreover, he was most upset at the defensive reactions of the teachers of the first Waldorf school in Stuttgart to the results of a school inspection from the local authorities; for instead of siding with the teachers, Steiner saw much truth in what the 'outside' authorities had criticized.

We ourselves have certainly met personalities and even practices in some Steiner institutions that make less than favourable impressions! The same is of course true for state institutions. We have also meet some of the most engaging, talented and down-to-earth personalities working as Steiner educators, and in other institutions – personalities who greatly enrich the lives of the children in their care and others in the community. The simple reality is that human beings are complex, diverse and difficult, but often work in a complementary way such that the strengths of the one balance out the difficult aspects of the other.

Finally, there are those who seem to scour Steiner's work looking for quotations and sentences that can be taken to 'prove' that he was in some form or other racist. In our considered view, there are a very few formulations scattered in some of his 6,000 lectures that one would not use today; and had he lectured today, he also would not have used them. However, the character of Steiner's work is fundamentally anti-racist (see House, 2013; Rose, 2013). As outlined, the individual human 'I' is something that transcends race, which is to be treated as entirely different to the physical body in which it temporarily resides. For Steiner, culture was a far more important influence than race: for example, he thought that human development preceded in cultural phases (e.g. the ancient Indian, Persian, Jewish, Greek cultures etc.). Although he believed that race played an important role in the distant past,[21] he utterly rejected racial distinctions in favour of individual distinctions in this age.

Two historical facts also support this position. First, the National Socialists in Germany closed Waldorf schools before the Second World War because they did not fit with racist Nazi ideology. However, far more relevant than the decrees of Himmler and Hitler are the founding statutes of the General Anthroposophical Society in 1923:

> Anyone can become a member, without regard to nationality, social
> standing, religion, scientific or artistic conviction, who considers
> as justified the existence of an institution such as the Goetheanum
> in Dornach, in its capacity as a School of Spiritual Science. The
> Anthroposophical Society rejects any kind of sectarian activity.
> *(Statute 4, General Anthroposophical Society, 1923)*

8.2 School readiness and early academic focus

Internationally, and almost without exception, pressure is exerted on children to accelerate their development in traditional academic skills (House, 2011). At one end of this spectrum, this pressure is a little more subtle, ranging from games designed to teach numeracy and literacy, exposure to learning software and electronically 'stimulating' toys, or pseudo-scientific explanations for everyday phenomena (e.g. how an electric light works). At the other end of the spectrum, pressure takes on more extreme forms still, such that play itself is under threat, being replaced with more 'learning' activities, state sanctioned and imposed from above (House, 2000, 2007, 2011). Over the course of time, the mantra 'start early, intervene early' has been patently misused, taken from areas in which it belongs – such as in language learning, medical illness and sensory development – and indiscriminately applied to the latest educational fad (e.g. phonics, alphabetical skills, computer skills). Subsequently, many Steiner teachers, kindergarten or otherwise, experience this pressure first-hand from parents and governments to do more to support and actively encourage reading and numeracy development in the early years. Examining the question from another angle: Why do Steiner kindergartens not also spend a small part of their time teaching children to read and count?

Paradoxically, Steiner kindergartens actually do teach children early literacy and numeracy skills. Beginning with reading, this skill is language in a symbolic form; visual in the case of normal reading, haptic and proprioceptive in the case of braille. Essentially, the foundation of reading is actually language, experienced through the senses. Underpinning the importance of language, we recently demonstrated that kindergarten children who can better understand and tell a story go on to have greater reading comprehension when they are 16 years old (Suggate et al., 2018). At a conceptual level, we require much longer to acquire the many thousands of words needed for language than we do to learn the 26 letters of the alphabet and their corresponding links to the sounds they make (Suggate, 2015). Given that early childhood minds are primed for learning language, it seems to make little sense to divert this plasticity towards the abstract symbols of reading.

Furthermore, work is showing that reading of letters, that is abstract symbols, involves the sensorimotor system (Suggate et al., 2016; Vinter and Chartrel, 2008; Wamain et al., 2012). We have also recently shown that children who first develop their fine motor skills tend to go on to become better readers after the beginning of school (Suggate et al., 2016). Like language, the brain in the early years seems primed to hone information derived from the senses, again giving rise to the question as to why we would want to distract from this important process. There is also evidence that reading requires the ability to create vivid mental images (Sadoski and Paivio, 2013). Children in the early years very much live in these mental images – their imaginative play can be seen as precisely schooling this faculty, in combination with their strong desire for sensorimotor interactions with the environment. Thus, through free story-telling, rich play interactions, artistic activities (which represent a first foray into the world of symbolism) and sensorimotor experiences, Steiner kindergartens do much to support the very foundations of literacy development.

The same also applies for mathematical development, which is also dependent on sensorimotor experience. To know mathematical concepts is to know the world: mathematical concepts are embedded everywhere in physical relations – in musical timing, in gravity, acceleration, mass, velocity estimations of moving objects, constructing physical structures, temperature estimations, and dividing up food. Children need to first learn how mathematical concepts feel, so that – as the ability for abstract thought later increases – these can be internalized into mathematical ideas. Here too, we have shown that early fine motor skills lead to later mathematical development (Fischer et al., 2017; Suggate et al., 2017). Again, Steiner kindergartens do much implicit teaching of early mathematics!

Finally, the most important reason to not explicitly teach early reading is that it is both useless and harmful (Suggate, 2011, 2012). Studies looking at the later reading of children starting early, at age 5, in comparison to later, at age 7, find that there is simply no advantage by about age 9 (Durkin, 1974–5; Elley, 1992; Suggate, 2009; Suggate, Schaughency and Reese, 2013). In fact, Steiner children seem to overtake their earlier starting state-school peers by about age 13 (Suggate, Schaughency and Reese, 2013). Early interventions targeting reading skills in kindergarten have very modest effects (Suggate, 2010) that basically wash out after as little as 11 months (Suggate, 2016). Early reading and formal school have been found to link to more problem behaviour in the first years of school (Magnusson et al., 2007; Marcon, 2002). One study found that poor children attending a kindergarten with an early academic focus had greater levels of social deviancy as teenagers (Schweinhart and Weikart, 1997). Most worryingly, gifted children who began school earlier soon lost their academic advantage, with this turning into more emotional crises in midlife, lesser life satisfaction, and an earlier death (Kern and Friedman, 2009).

Taken together there is simply little scientific evidence to make a compelling case that children should learn explicit reading skills in kindergarten. Instead, the picture seems to support a fundamental principle of Steiner education – namely, that misdirecting the early forces of growth, sensory experience, imitation and imagination is counter-beneficial in the long-term.

8.3 Electronic media

Steiner early years education is universally free of electronic media, meaning that there are no televisions, computers or other screen devices in kindergarten rooms. Indeed, there are often few electrical devices in kindergarten at all, as outlined earlier, because preference is given to directly observable mechanical processes (section 6.4.1). Thus, for example, grains are prepared by grinding them with a hand-mill, so that the children can participate in and directly perceive the preparation process. However, this position is often taken as indicating retrogressive, even anti-progressive, or anti-technology tendencies. Some arguments go so far as to claim that by not offering children experiences with electronic media, important educational experiences are being withheld.

The first misconception that we would like to address is the idea that Steiner education does not work with media. Instead, a nuanced approach to media is taken, in which these are seen as being a fairly recent, but highly important, cultural development. By definition, a medium acts as an intermediary between that which it represents and the partaker. Phenomenologically speaking, media stand in the way between the real 'things' of this world and those experiencing these. As such, media represent an impoverished representation of reality, through the subjective world of the creator of the medial matter. This has important consequences, because a direct phenomenological observation is no longer possible: instead, one gains access to reality through the eyes of the other. Accordingly, it is important at some stage for children to learn to realise that media are not reality but representations thereof; and media education therefore needs to be offered to convey this. But how?

The first media that humankind experienced were probably symbolic drawings, out of which symbolic writing and then alphabetic writing systems developed (Rose, 2007). Originally written by hand, the printing press overtook production of books and print media. At the end of the nineteenth century, new forms of media were possible after the invention of the gramophone and the first video cameras, now digital devices, handheld devices, and increasingly 'augmented' and three-dimensional 'reality' media have been developed.

As emphasized throughout this book, but especially in Chapters 4 and 5, the developing human being has an enormous but crucial task to carry out – namely, the development of the senses. To recapitulate, the development of the senses is vital for the perception of a number of qualities alongside thought and healthy judgement. The approach taken in Steiner education is to couple the exposure to media to children's development so that it initially supports, instead of undermining, the developing human being. In the early years, media experiences are offered through drawing with (thick) crayons and also water-colour painting.

Both of these media are deemed suitable for a number of reasons. First, children have to work wilfully with the crayons to create a result. Unlike felt pens that fill the paper with minimal effort, crayons require 'elbow grease', which again develops the will. Secondly, both these media offer a great degree of transparency, children can see how the colour affects the paper directly, and colours can be mixed and overridden. Drawing on an electronic device does not offer this rich tapestry of experience and sensory stimulation (e.g. smell, warmth, texture): rather, visual and auditory modalities dominate. Thirdly, drawing and water colours generally result in aesthetically pleasing work regardless of initial skill level, which is rewarding and formative for children.

After being exposed to the more directly perceptible media in the early years, in Steiner schools the transition to written and other media is made in the primary school years (see section 7.4). Often, children work with sound media in the middle school classes (around age 10), perhaps recording a story. In the upper school, children are thought to have enjoyed a sufficient preparation in non-digital media to then be able to transition to the digital media.

Turning to harm, there is a large and growing body of evidence indicating that negative effects of digital media exist. The first area of concern is the artificial light source emitted from electronic media. Humans depend on daily doses of natural light for health, including regulating bodily rhythms (Skeldon et al., 2017). Disruption to this is associated with medical and psychological disorders (Gooley et al., 2011; Vandewalle et al., 2007). Exposure to electronic media, especially but not exclusively in the evenings, disturbs sleep and memory (Chang et al., 2015; Dworak et al., 2007). Given the importance of sleep in learning – especially for the developing child – it is not advisable to expose children to digital media when young. Clearly, this is not a position that all households will adopt, which makes it all the more important that the kindergarten day begins with an electronic media-free zone, and exposure to natural light and nature.

A second danger that accompanies electronic media is that of addiction. For some reason, electronic media are highly addictive (Yuan et al., 2011). Although some people are able to interact with digital devices and experience minimal interest, or perhaps even total disinterest, the majority experience addiction symptoms, and many experience addiction to the level of pathology. Pathological effects include disruption to daily life, preoccupation with media, neglect of duties, relationships, health and self-care (Lepp et al., 2015; Yang et al., 2013). Adults clearly struggle to disengage, and children who have much lesser self-control and ability to inhibit their behaviour can be expected to be even more susceptible to addictive effects.

Thirdly, it is questionable as to what educational benefit is derived from electronic media in childhood. Experimental evidence indicates that children have great difficulty learning new words from video, with learning from peers and adults proving superior (Krcmar et al., 2007; Rosebury et al., 2009). Evidence indicates that children's language development is delayed if they have too much screen time in the early years (Zimmerman et al., 2007). Attempts to develop video games to improve reading skills have been disappointing (Łuniewska et al., 2018).

Further negative effects of electronic media consumption have been found in terms of aggression (Anderson et al., 2010). General cognitive development, as measured by intelligence tests also appears to suffer to some degree from a high exposure to screen time in the first three years of life (Zimmerman and Christakis, 2005). Academic achievement is negatively affected by screen time (Hancox et al., 2005; Weis and Cerankosky, 2010). Children's ability to attend to information and initiate and inhibit actions appears to suffer if exposed to fast-paced media (Lillard and Peterson, 2011; Nikkelen et al., 2014). However, video game play can also lead to faster processing of stimuli in the visual field over the short term (Anguera et al., 2013) – pointing to its generally stimulating effect.

A new field of research is required that examines whether children's sensory development is affected by electronic media. There is the well-known video deficit effect, whereby children have trouble inferring three-dimensional space from two-dimensional screens (Zack et al., 2009). To date, there are indications that screen time affects fine motor development (Cadoret et al., 2017), obesity and physical development (Fitzpatrick et al., 2012). Also, visual problems can result from excessive screen time (Bener et al., 2010).

Finally, there is no doubt that play is also affected by screen time. The presence of a running television reduces engagement in play, even if children only periodically view the screen media (Schmidt et al., 2008). Play becomes dominated by the themes experienced through the media (Valkenburg and van der Voort, 1995). On the balance of evidence, it appears that television viewing might increase day-dreaming but decrease creative imagination (Valkenburg and van der Voort, 1994).

In summary, although there has been much speculation and even scaremongering about the effects of media – also in Steiner education – there do appear to be robust, research-based indications that these can indeed harm children's sleep, learning, memory, attention spans, physical development, creative imagination, language and cognitive development. For this reason, the Steiner approach to media education, beginning with an introduction to drawing and painting in the early years, would seem to be advisable.

8.4 Modern and yet Steiner

The foundations of Steiner education and the very first kindergartens and schools were mostly developed shortly after the First World War, with the establishment of the vast majority of schools and kindergartens occurring after the Second World War (see sections 2.4 and 7.1). The inspiration for the development of the educational principles derives from Steiner's descriptions of the being of man (see Chapter 3). An impressive development of methods, collections of stories, fairy tales and rhymes, the selection and development of craft and art materials, the advent of toys and activities, and appropriate festival celebrations have been pioneered by many since Steiner's time. An increasing body of scientific evidence, as we have tried to outline throughout, now supports much of the educational approach. In Germany and the rest of Europe, the post-war period brought growth in Steiner education, which has not only not abated, but has migrated around the world, including to the Far East, where this method is currently being enthusiastically received.

However, a number of challenges face the further development of this educational approach. Perhaps most pressing is the shortage of Steiner-trained teachers. The Steiner movement as a whole needs to ask itself carefully and openly, why is there a shortage of educators? Is this due to the quality of training centres or associated costs, the difficulty and remuneration of the job, or simply that too few feel called into this profession? The natural consequence of this shortfall in trained Steiner teachers is that many state-trained personnel now work in Steiner settings. This can potentially bring new colleagues with fresh ideas and enthusiasm for an alternative approach, but can also create difficulty in retaining an authentic Steiner-Waldorf character.

Alongside changes in teaching personnel, there have also been marked societal and familial changes. The shift in family life, from two-parent to more single-parent homes and from home to institutionalized care, brings challenges, with an increasing amount of foundational work raising children being carried out by non-primary caregivers.

Children too appear to be changing. Many parents and teachers report that small children are more alert and sensitive than previously, and it has also been suggested that both sleep quality and duration have decreased over the last 50 years (Youngstedt et al., 2016). New challenges include an aging population, an epidemic of (childhood) mental and medical illness (including obesity, and anxiety, attention and language disorders), and an estrangement from nature. As mentioned above, electronic media and government academic requirements also detract from child-centred educational work.

150

How well equipped is the Steiner approach to deal with such challenges? How can Steiner education work within society, without detaching itself from it, yet still protect childhood? With this book, we hope to convey that although Steiner education may not have all the answers to these problems, the broad approach and profound philosophical foundation – coupled with the call for teachers to continually reflect on themselves and their work so as better to understand not only themselves, but each individual child – provides a good basis. In all likelihood, Steiner education needs to offer both remedies and pragmatism in the face of challenges.

In a Nutshell

- Steiner-Waldorf education faces a number of challenges, from within and from without.

- Challenges relate to misconceptions about religion and spirituality, early readiness and academic learning, and electronic media.

- Educators need to be open to children from all corners of society and adjust their approach to meet the needs of those in their care.

- Steiner-Waldorf educators also need to be self-aware and self-critical regarding their ability to respond and adapt, being receptive to other approaches and new impulses.

Footnotes

1　Which, as discussed in section 5.2.1, would perhaps have been more accurately translated as 'The philosophy of freehood'!

2　Constructivism is a philosophical position which maintains that we construct our own worlds ourselves, therefore there is no objective truth, but only our subjective experience. In education, constructivism means approaches whereby children are more actively engaged in learning. Because knowledge is constructed, children need to be active in constructing this, and not sitting in front of a teacher just memorizing, for example.

3　Depending on how one divides up the various systems, it is possible to derive four or seven, because none of the qualities is completely separate; rather, they permeate one another. For the sake of completion, the fourth principle, the 'I', is intimately connected with the blood, including its circulation.

4　Steiner actually suggested actively making small changes to habits as a way to strengthen the will (e.g. changing one's handwriting).

5　We are grateful to Michael Errenst, who compiled Steiner's quotations on the various senses in his manuscript 'Die zwölf Sinne im Werk Rudolf Steiners und die Anthroposophie'.

6　Il est droit, parce que Taxe de son corps en longueur, prolongement d'un rayon de notre globe, est perpendiculaire au plan d'horizon. Il est tourné vers le ciel, parce que la direction de cet axe lui indique le Zénith précisément au dessus du sommet de la tête: deux caractères contenu simplicitement l'un dans l'autre, et rigoureusement distinctifs. C'est donc, comme du centre de la terre que l'Homme semble s'élever jusqu'à la voûte des cieux, et remplir tout l'entre-deux de ces extrêmes. Sa force et sa dignité physiques, résultantes de sa marche droite, deviennent comme les garants de sa force et de sa dignité morales, et voilà tout l'Homme compris dans l'expression de son propre Axe, seule et unique direction verticale primitive et absolue.

7　Retrieved 20 March 2019 from: poetry in translation.com/PITBR/ German/Heine.php.

8　Just for the sake of clarity, our position is not exactly this one, but that only when specific thoughts are being perceived are they, in a sense, part of the mind.

9　In the words of Steiner: 'When you confront another person something like the following happens. You perceive a person for a short time and he or she makes an impression on you. This impression disturbs you inwardly; you feel that the person, who is really a similar being to yourself, and this makes an impression on you, like an attack. The result is that you "defend" yourself in your inner being, that you oppose yourself to this attack, that you become inwardly aggressive towards him or her. This feeling then abates, and your aggression ceases; hence he or she can now make another impression upon you. Then your aggressive force has time to rise again, and again you have an aggressive feeling. Once more it abates, and the other makes a fresh impression upon you – and so on. That is the relationship which exists when one person meets another and perceives his or her ego: giving yourself up to the other human being – inwardly warding him off; giving yourself up again – warding him off; sympathy – antipathy; sympathy – antipathy. I am not now speaking of the feeling life, but of what takes place in perception when you confront a man. The soul vibrates: sympathy – antipathy; sympathy – antipathy.' (Steiner 1919/1993, translation adapted from wn.rsarchive.org)

10   In Steiner's literature, 'intellectual' often refers to abstract cold thinking, devoid of reality. The word 'intellectual' is here meant as that which refers to ideas and entities that can be thought or perceived and investigated with the mind (thoughts such as mathematical concepts, laws, categories, archetypes), but need not be abstract and cold.

11   To our knowledge, Michael Wilson first made this distinction in his translation of Steiner's book *The Philosophy of Freedom*.

12   Although a bit clichéd, there is a nice joke that gets at the difference between freedom and freehood, as understood in the German and English cultures. In the United States in particular, freedom means doing whatever you want to do; in Germany, freedom means doing whatever you are allowed to do!

13   Steiner used the word 'authority'. The word 'authority' creates misunderstanding today because it is associated with authoritarianism; however, in our view Steiner's concept of 'authority' is better approximated in this context by the word 'relationship'.

14   'The Rubicon' refers to an important milestone in Steiner's developmental psychology. The Rubicon is a river north of Rome from which, once attacking armies had crossed, there was no going back. Similarly, children who cross the Rubicon reach a point in their individual development from which there is also no going back. Specifically, this developmental step occurs in middle childhood around age 9, and is associated with a greater degree of independence from the parents because a greater degree of 'I' consciousness has been attained.

15   This is called the 'binding problem'.

16   Steiner used the term 'percept', not sensation, to refer to the elementary sense perception 'something is there'. Today, the term sensation is more commonly used to express the idea for which Steiner used the term 'percept'.

17   For example, Steiner was a vocal opponent of Woodrow Wilson's ideas on national self-determination, because he thought this would lead to further and endless division based on a false principle. Instead, he argued for something that would be seen today as universal human rights which, when upheld, allow peoples of all races, religions and cultures to exist within nation states.

18   This criticism applies to this book! However, in our experience, it is a mistake trying to re-create Steiner's style, for several reasons. First, when authors do this, as in much anthroposophical literature, the result is often not the effect that Steiner created with his writing, but rather one of dogmatism. Secondly, modern consciousness is different: there is a need amongst many for this precise and clear style of writing, particularly in the English-speaking world. Finally, we have to write in a way that is to us authentic.

19   Eurythmy is a form of moving art that seeks to embody forms, archetypes, speech, moods and inner gestures through visible, holistic movement. Not only is it practised as an art form, it has educative and even curative applications too, as it helps shape the human body to become a tool of the individual human, thereby working against the often-prevalent mechanizing and disembodying influences today. Some have likened it to a European Thai-Chi. Eurythmy was invented by Rudolf Steiner and his wife, Marie Steiner.

20   Not many Montessori teachers today would adhere to this idea that imaginative play is harmful.

21   Any proponent of evolutionary theory is actually, strictly speaking, racist, seeing all human faculties as being anchored in genes. For Steiner, genes (and hence race) constitute just one influence amongst many.

References

Allanson, A. & Teensma, N. (2018). Writing to reading the Steiner Waldorf way: Foundations of creative literacy in classes 1 and 2. Stroud: Hawthorn Press.

American Psychiatric Association. (2009). Diagnostic and statistical manual of mental disorders: DSM-IV-TR (4th edn, text revision, 13. print). Arlington, VA: American Psychiatric Association.

Anderson, C. A., Shibuya, A., Ihori, N., & others (2010). Violent video game effects on aggression, empathy, and prosocial behavior in Eastern and Western countries: A meta-analytic review. Psychological Bulletin, 136 (2), 151–173.

Anguera, J. A., Boccanfuso, J., Rintoul, J. L., & others (2013). Video game training enhances cognitive control in older adults. Nature, 501 (7465), 97–101.

Aristotle. (2003). Nikomachische Ethik (Bibliogr. erg. Ausg). Universal-Bibliothek: Nr. 8586. Stuttgart: Reclam.

Barsalou, L. W. (2008). Grounded cognition. Annual Review of Psychology, 59 (1), 617–645.

Barsalou, L. W. (2010). Grounded cognition: Past, present, and future. Topics in Cognitive Science, 2 (4), 716–724.

Bener, A., Al-Mahdi, H. S., Vachhani, P. J., Al-Nufal, M., & Ali, A. I. (2010). Do excessive internet use, television viewing and poor lifestyle habits affect low vision in school children? Journal of Child Health Care, 14 (4), 375–385.

Berardi, N., Pizzorusso, T., & Maffei, L. (2000). Critical periods during sensory development. Current Opinion in Neurobiology, 10 (1), 138–145. Berk, L. E. (2004). Child development (6th edn [Nachdr.]). Boston, Mass.: Allyn and Bacon.

Bischof, N. (2014). Psychologie: Ein Grundkurs für Anspruchsvolle [The foundations of psycholgy for the critical] (3. Aufl.). Stuttgart: Kohlhammer.

Blanche, E. I., Bodison, S., Chang, M. C., & Reinoso, G. (2012). Development of the comprehensive observations of proprioception (COP): Validity, reliability, and factor analysis. American Journal of Occupational Therapy, 66 (6), 691–698.

Bradley, R. M., & Mistretta, C. M. (1975). Fetal sensory receptors. Physiological Reviews, 55, 352–382.

Brandwein, A. B., Foxe, J. J., Russo, N. N., Altschuler, T. S., Gomes, H., & Molholm, S. (2011). The development of audiovisual multisensory integration across childhood and early adolescence: A high-density electrical mapping study. Cerebral Cortex 21 (5), 1042–1055; available at goo.gl/PYDahD (accessed 8 October 2018).

Bund der freien Waldorfschulen, (2018). Author. www.waldorfschule.de/ (accessed 26 July 2018).

Cadoret, G., Bigras, N., Lemay, L., Lehrer, J., & Lemire, J. (2017). Relationship between screen-time and motor proficiency in children: A longitudinal study. Early Child Development and Care, 18, 1–9.

Cahn, S. M. (Ed.). (2009). Philosophy of education: The essential texts. New York: Routledge.

Carr, D. (2012). On the educational value of moral virtues: Some lessons from ancient philosophy. In S. P. Suggate & E. Reese (Eds.), Contemporary debates in child development and education (pp. 307–315). London: Routledge.

Carr, L., Iacoboni, M., Dubeau, M.-C., Mazziotta, J. C., & Lenzi, G. L. (2003). Neural mechanisms of empathy in humans: A relay from neural systems for imitation to limbic areas. Proceedings of the National Academy of Sciences of the United States of America, 100 (9), 5497–5502.

Chang, A.-M., Aeschbach, D., Duffy, J. F., & Czeisler, C. A. (2015). Evening use of light-emitting eReaders negatively affects sleep, circadian timing, and next-morning alertness. Proceedings of the National Academy of Sciences of the United States of America, 112 (4), 1232–1237.

Compani, M.-L. (Ed.). (2011). Waldorfkindergarten heute: Eine Einführung (1. Aufl). Stuttgart: Verl. Freies Geistesleben.

Dabelea, D., Mayer-Davis, E. J., Saydah, S., & others (2014). Prevalence of type 1 and type 2 diabetes among children and adolescents from 2001 to 2009. Journal of the American Medical Association, 311 (17), 1778–1786.

Dahlin, B. (2009). On the path towards thinking: Learning from Martin Heidegger and Rudolf Steiner. Studies in Philosophy and Education, 28 (6), 537–554.

Dahlin, B. (2012). The purpose of education – a 'post-liberal' perspective. In S. P. Suggate & E. Reese (Eds.), Contemporary debates in child development and education (pp. 3–12). London: Routledge.

Decety, J. & Meyer, M. (2008). From emotion resonance to empathic understanding: A social developmental neuroscience account. Development and Psychopathology, 20 (4), 1053–1080.

Descartes, R. (Ed.). (2012). Discours de la méthode pour bien conduiresaraison et chercher la véritédanslessciences: Französisch/deutsch – Bericht über die Methode, die Vernunft richtig zu führen und die Wahrheit in den Wissenschaften zu erforschen ([Nachdr.]). Reclams Universal-Bibliothek: Nr. 18100. Stuttgart: Reclam.

Diesendruck, G. (2009). Mechanisms of word learning. In E. Hoff & M. Shatz (Eds.), Blackwell handbook of language development (pp. 257–276). Chichester: Wiley-Blackwell.

Douillard, J. (2017). Eat wheat: A scientific and clinically proven approach to safely bringing wheat and dairy back into your diet. New York: Morgan James Publishing.

Drummond, M. J. (2011). The work of the teacher: Key themes and absences. In R. Parker-Rees (Ed.), Meeting the child in Steiner kindergartens: An exploration of beliefs, values, and practices (pp. 94–102). London: Routledge.

Drummond, M. J. & Jenkinson, S. (n.d.). Meeting the child: Approaches to observation and assessment in Steiner kindergartens. Plymouth: University of Plymouth.

Dunn, W., Griffith, J. W., Sabata, D., & others (2015). Measuring change in somatosensation across the lifespan. American Journal of Occupational Therapy, 69 (3), 6903290020p1–9.

Durkin, D. (1974–1975). A six year study of children who learned to read in school at the age of four. Reading Research Quarterly, 10, 9–61.

Dworak, M., Schierl, T., Bruns, T., & Strüder, H. K. (2007). Impact of singular excessive computer game and television exposure on sleep patterns and memory performance of school-aged children. Pediatrics, 120 (5), 978–985.

Ebbeling, C. B., Pawlak, D. B., & Ludwig, D. S. (2002). Childhood obesity: Public-health crisis, common sense cure. The Lancet, 360 (9331), 473–482.

Edwards, C. P. (2007). Three approaches from Europe: Waldorf, Montessori, and Reggio Emilia. Early Childhood Research and Practice, 4 (1); available at goo.gl/W1LLBs (accessed 8 October 2018).

Elley, W. B. (1992). How in the world do students read? IEA study of reading literacy. The Hague, Netherlands: International Association for the Evaluation of Educational Achievement.

Ely, R., & McCabe, A. (1994). The language play of kindergarten children. First Language, 14, 19–35.

Ernst, M. O. (2008). Multisensory integration: A late bloomer. Current Biology, 18 (12), R519–521.

Filippetti, M. L., Johnson, M. H., Lloyd-Fox, S., Dragovic, D., & Farroni, T. (2013). Body perception in newborns. Current Biology, 23, 2413–2416.

Fischer, U., Suggate, S. P., Schmirl, J., & Stoeger, H. (2018). Counting on fine motor skills: Links between preschool finger dexterity and numerical skills. Developmental Science, 21(4), /e12623.

Fitzpatrick, C., Pagani, L. S., & Barnett, T. A. (2012). Early childhood television viewing predicts explosive leg strength and waist circumference by middle childhood. International Journal of Behavioral Nutrition and Physical Activity, 9, 87.

Fließbach, A., Mäder, P., Pfiffner, L., Dubois D., & Gunst, L. (2000). Organic farming enhances soil fertility and biodiversity: Results from a 21 year old field trial. FiBL Dossier 1. Research Institute of Organic Agriculture (FiBL); available at goo.gl/pxC4NX (accessed 8 October 2018).

Forster, L. W. (1990). The Penguin book of German verse. Harmondsworth: Penguin.

Frankl, V. E. (2008). Man's search for meaning. London: Rider (orig. 1973).

Fulkerson, M. (2014). Rethinking the senses and their interactions: The case for sensory pluralism. Frontiers in Psychology, 5, 1426.

Fuster, J. M. (2002). Frontal lobe and cognitive development. Journal of Neurocytology, 31, 373–385.

Gallagher, M. & Ferrè, E. R. (2018). The aesthetics of verticality: A gravitational contribution to aesthetic preference. Quarterly Journal of Experimental Psychology, 22 January; available at goo.gl/ixVnAN (accessed 8 October 2018).

Gallagher, S. (2006). How the body shapes the mind (1st pb edn). Oxford: Clarendon Press.

Gallagher, S. and Cole, J. (1995). Body schema and body image in a deafferented subject. Journal of Mind and Behavior, 16, 369–390; reprinted in D. Welton (Ed.), Body and flesh: A philosophical reader (pp. 131–147), Oxford: Blackwell, 2010.

Gallese, V. (2013). Mirror neurons and the perception–action link. In K. N. Ochsner & S. Kosslyn (Eds.), The Oxford handbook of cognitive neuroscience, Volume 1 (pp. 244–256). Oxford: Oxford University Press.

Gallistel, C. R. & Balsam, P. D. (2014). Time to rethink the neural mechanisms of learning and memory. Neurobiology of Learning and Memory, 108, 136–144.

Goddard Blythe, S. (2011). Physical foundations for learning. In R. House (Ed.), Too much, too soon? Early learning and the erosion of childhood (pp. 131–146). Stroud: Hawthorn Press.

Goddard Blythe, S. (2018). Movement: Your child's first language. Stroud: Hawthorn Press.

Goethe, J. W. (1810/1840). Goethe's theory of colours. London: John Murray.

Goldstein, W. (2000). Experimental proof for the effects of biodynamic preparations. Biodynamics, 231, 6–13.

Golinkoff, R. M., Hirsh-Pasek, K., & Singer, D. G. (2006). Why play = learning: A challenge for parents and educators. In D. G. Singer, R. M. Golinkoff & K. Hirsh-Pasek (Eds.), Play = learning: How play motivates and enhances children's cognitive and social-emotional growth (pp. 3–12). Oxford: Oxford University Press.

Gooley, J. J., Chamberlain, K., Smith, K. A., & others (2011). Exposure to room light before bedtime suppresses melatonin onset and shortens melatonin duration in humans. Journal of Clinical Endocrinology and Metabolism, 96 (3), E463–E472.

Gori, M., Del Viva, M., Sandini, G., & Burr, D. C. (2008). Young children do not integrate visual and haptic form information. Current Biology, 18 (9), 694–698.

Goulardins, J. B., Marques, J. C. B., Casella, E. B., Nascimento, R. O., & Oliveira, J. A. (2013). Motor profile of children with attention deficit hyperactivity disorder, combined type. Research in Developmental Disabilities, 34 (1), 40–45.

Grunelius, von, E. M. (1950/1991). Early childhood education and the Waldorf School Plan, Waldorf curriculum series. [Place of publication not identified]: Rudolf Steiner College Publications.

Grunelius, von, E. (1993). Rudolf Steiner asks for kindergartens. In J. Almon (Ed.), An overview of the Waldorf Kindergarten (vol. 1). Silver Spring, MD: Waldorf Kindergarten Association.

Hahn, H. (1930/1988). Vom Ernst des Spielens: Eine zeitgemässe Betrachtung über Spielzeug und Spiel [On the seriousness of play] (4th edn). Stuttgart: Mellinger.

Hall, S., Rumney, L., Holler, J., & Kidd, E. (2013). Associations among play, gesture and early spoken language acquisition. First Language, 33, 294–312.

Han, J., Waddington, G., Adams, R., Anson, J., & Liu, Y. (2016). Assessing proprioception: A critical review of methods. Journal of Sport and Health Science, 5 (1), 80–90.

Hancox, R. J., Milne, B. J., & Poulton, R. (2005). Association of television viewing during childhood with poor educational achievement. Archives of Pediatric Adolescent Medicine, 159, 614–618.

Hensel, H. (1998). Goethe, science, and sensory experience. In D. Seamon & A. Zajonc (Eds.), Goethe's way of science: A phenomenology of nature (pp. 71–82). Albany: State University of New York Press.

Heyes, C. (2001). Causes and consequences of imitation. Trends in Cognitive Sciences, 5, 253–261.

Hildreth, L. (2006). The Waldorf Kindergarten snack book (1st edn). Massachusetts: Bell Pond Books.

House, R. (2000). Stress, surveillance and modernity: The 'modernising' assault on our education system. Education Now: News and Review, 30 (Winter), Feature Supplement, 4 pp.

House. R. (2006). Beyond materialistic education: Steiner (Waldorf) education for the evolution of human consciousness. In V. Nolan & G. Darby (Eds.), Reinventing education: A thought experiment… (pp. 123–34), Stoke Mandeville, Aylesbury: Synectics Education Initiative; edited version in New View, 40 (July–Sept.), 2006, 62–66.

House, R. (2007). Schooling, the state and children's psychological well-being: A psychosocial critique. Journal of Psychosocial Research, 2 (July–Dec), 49–62.

House, R. (Ed.). (2011). Too much, too soon? Early learning and the erosion of childhood. Stroud: Hawthorn Press.

House, R. (2013). A refutation of the allegation of racism against Rudolf Steiner. New View magazine, Summer; available online at goo.gl/ZVYo18 (accessed 4 October 2018).

House, R. & Loewenthal, D. (Eds.) (2008). Against and for CBT: Towards a constructive dialogue. Ross-on-Wye: PCCS Books.

Humbert de Superville, D. P. G. (1827). Essai sur les signes inconditionnels dans l'art; available at goo.gl/MXCLYQ (accessed 8 October 2018).

Huth, A. G., Heer, W. A. de, Griffiths, T. L., Theunissen, F. E., & Gallant, J. L. (2016). Natural speech reveals the semantic maps that tile human cerebral cortex. Nature, 532 (7600), 453–458.

Jacobs, D. R. & Steffen, L. M. (2003). Nutrients, foods, and dietary patterns as exposures in research: A framework for food synergy. American Journal of Clinical Nutrition, 78, 508S–513S.

Jenkinson, S. (2011). Reading the book of the child: The Steiner teacher's inner work and its relation to child observation. In R. Parker-Rees (Ed.), Meeting the child in Steiner kindergartens: An exploration of beliefs, values, and practices (pp. 103–116). London: Routledge.

Jensen, J. J. & Langsted, O. (2004). Dänemark: Pädagogische Qualität ohne nationales Curriculum. In W. E. Fthenakis & P. Oberhuemer (Eds.), Frühpädagogik international: Bildungsqualität im Blickpunkt (pp. 191–207). Wiesbaden, p.l.: VS Verlag für Sozialwissenschaften.

Kagerer, F. A. & Clark, J. E. (2015). Development of kinesthetic-motor and auditory-motor representations in school-aged children. Experimental Brain Research, 233 (7), 2181–2194.

Kassner, M. (2011). Ernährung im Kindergarten heute. In M.-L. Compani (Ed.), Waldorfkindergarten heute: Eine Einführung [Waldorfkindergartens today] (1st edn) (pp. 215–232). Stuttgart: Verlag Freies Geistesleben.

Kern, M. L. & Friedman, H. S. (2009). Early educational milestones as predictors of lifelong academic achievement, midlife adjustment, and longevity. Journal of Applied Developmental Psychology, 30 (4), 419–430.

Kley-Auerswald, M. (2017). Das Montessori-Kinderhaus (1st edn). Freiburg: Herder Verlag. Retrieved 6 October 2018 from https://ebookcentral. proquest.com/lib/gbv/detail.action?docID=4933114

Kley-Auerswald, M. & Schmutzler, H.-J. (2015). Montessori (1. Aufl.). Frühe Kindheit pädagogische Ansätze für die Kita. Berlin: Cornelsen.

Knobeloch, L., Salna, B., Hogan, A., Postle, J., & Anderson, H. (2000). Blue babies and nitrate-contaminated well water. Environmental Health Perspectives, 108, 675–678.

Konicarova, J. & Bob, P. (2012). Retained primitive reflexes and ADHD in children. Activitas Nervosa Superior, 54 (3–4), 135–138.

Kosslyn, S. M., Margolis, J. A., Barrett, A. M., Goldknopf, E. J., & Daly, P. F. (1990). Age differences in imagery abilities. Child Development, 61 (4), 995.

Krcmar, M., Grela, B., & Lin, K. (2007). Can toddlers learn vocabulary from television? An experimental approach. Media Psychology, 10, 41–63.

Kutzli, R. (2007). Creative form drawing. Stroud: Hawthorn Press.

Labaree, D. (2014). Let's measure what no one teaches: PISA, NCLB, and the shrinking aims of education. Teacher's College Record, 116, 1–14.

Lakoff, G. & Johnson, M. (2010). Philosophy in the flesh: The embodied mind and its challenge to Western thought. New York: Basic Books.

Lang, P. (2011). Erziehung im Vorschulalter: Salutogenese und Kompetenzbildung. In M.-L. Compani (Ed.), Waldorfkindergarten heute: Eine Einführung (1st edn) (pp. 34–64). Stuttgart: Verl. Freies Geistesleben.

Leber, S. (1997). Anthroposophie und Waldorfpädagogik in den Kulturen der Welt: Porträts aus elf Ländern und zwei grundlegende Beiträge [Anthroposophy and Waldorf education in the cultures of the world] (1st edn). Stuttgart: Verlag Freies Geistesleben.

Lenhart, J., Lenhard, W., Vaahtoranta, E., & Suggate, S. P. (2018). More than words: Narrator engagement during storytelling increases children's word learning, story comprehension, and on-task behavior. Journal of Educational Psychology, Manuscript submitted for publication.

Lepp, A., Barkley, J. E., & Karpinski, A. C. (2015). The relationship between cell phone use and academic performance in a sample of U.S. college students. SAGE Open, 5 (1), 215824401557316.

Levine, S. C., Ratliff, K. R., Huttenlocher, J., & Cannon, J. (2012). Early puzzle play: A predictor of preschoolers' spatial transformation skill. Developmental Psychology, 48 (2), 530–542.

Lewis, C. S. (2010a). The abolition of man, or, Reflections on education with special reference to the teaching of English in the upper forms of schools. Las Vegas: Lits.

Lewis, C. S. (2010b). The voyage of the dawn treader. The chronicles of Narnia: Vol. 5. London: HarperCollins.

Lewkowicz, D. J. (2000). The development of intersensory temporal perception: An epigenetic systems/limitations view. Psychological Bulletin, 126 (2), 281–308.

Lievegoed, B. (1985). Man on the threshold: The challenge of inner development. Stroud: Hawthorn Press.

Lievegoed, B. C. J. (2005). Phases of childhood (rev. edn). Edinburgh: Floris Books.

Lillard, A. S. (2013). Playfull learning and Montessori education. American Journal of Play, 5, 157–186.

Lillard, A. & Else-Quest, N. (2006). Evaluating Montessori education. Science, 313, 1893–1894.

Lillard, A. S. & Peterson, J. (2011). The immediate impact of different types of television on young children's executive function. Pediatrics, 128 (4), 644–649.

Lin, C.-H., Lien, Y.-H., Wang, S.-F., & Tsauo, J.-Y. (2006). Hip and knee proprioception in elite, amateur, and novice tennis players. American Journal of Physical Medicine and Rehabilitation, 85 (3), 216–221.

Lindenberg, C. (1997). Rudolf Steiner: Eine Biographie (1. Aufl). Stuttgart: Verl. Freies Geistesleben.

Lingenauber, S. (Ed.). (2011). Handlexikon der Reggio-Pädagogik (4., erw. Aufl.). Bochum: Projekt-Verl.

Liu, J., Wang, X.-Q., Zheng, J.-J., & others (2012). Effects of Tai Chi versus proprioception exercise program on neuromuscular function of the ankle in elderly people: A randomized controlled trial. Evidence-based Complementary and Alternative Medicine, Article ID 265486, 8pp.

Łuniewska, M., Chyl, K., Dębska, A., & others (2018). Neither action nor phonological video games make dyslexic children read better. Scientific Reports, 8 (1), 549.

McKeen, C. (2011). Die Metamorphose von Wachstumskräften in Denkkräfte. In M.-L. Compani (Ed.), Waldorfkindergarten heute: Eine Einführung (1st edn) (pp. 65–80). Stuttgart: Verl. Freies Geistesleben.

McNeil, M. C., Polloway, E. A., & Smith, J. D. (1984). Feral and isolated children: Historical review and analysis. Education and Training of the Mentally Retarded, February, 70–79.

McPhillips, M. & Sheehy, N. (2004). Prevalence of persistent primary reflexes and motor problems in children with reading difficulties. Dyslexia, 10 (4), 316–338.

Magnusson, K. A., Ruhm, C., & Waldfogel, J. (2007). Does kindergarten improve school preparation and performance? Economics of Education Review, 26, 33–51.

Marcon, R. A. (2002). Moving up the grades: Relationship between preschool model and later school success. Early Childhood Research & Practice, 4 (1); available at goo.gl/nzJvVv (accessed 8 October 2018).

Mast, F. W. (2014). Visceromotor sensation and control. In K. N. Ochsner & S. M. Kosslyn (Eds.), The Oxford handbook of cognitive neuroscience, Volume 2: The cutting edges (pp. 114–121). Oxford: Oxford University Press.

Michel, E., Roethlisberger, M., Neuenschwander, R., & Roebers, C. M. (2011). Development of cognitive skills in children with motor coordination impairments at 12 month follow-up. Child Neuropsychology, 17, 151–172.

Miklitz, I. (2016). Der Waldkindergarten: Dimensionen eines pädagogischen Ansatzes (6. Auflage). Frühe Kindheit Pädagogische Ansätze. Berlin: Cornelsen.

Molnar-Szakacs, I. (2011). From actions to empathy and morality – a neural perspective. Journal of Economic Behavior and Organization, 77 (1), 76–85.

Murray, G. K., Veijola, J., Moilanen, K., & others (2006). Infant motor development is associated with adult cognitive categorisation in a longitudinal birth cohort study. Journal of Child Psychology and Psychiatry, and Allied Disciplines, 47 (1), 25–29.

Neuffer, H. (Ed.). (2008). Zum Unterricht des Klassenlehrers an der Waldorfschule: Ein Kompendium (3., erw. u. überarb. Aufl.). Menschenkunde und Erziehung: Vol. 71. Stuttgart: Verl. Freies Geistesleben.

Nicol, J. (2011). Doing is learning: The domestic arts and artistic activities. In R. Parker-Rees (Ed.), Meeting the child in Steiner kindergartens: An exploration of beliefs, values, and practices (pp. 68–80). London: Routledge.

Nicol, J. (2016). Bringing the Steiner Waldorf approach to your early years practice (3rd edn). Abingdon, Oxon: Routledge.

Nicol, J. & Taplin, J. (2012). Understanding the Steiner Waldorf approach: Early years education in practice. Abingdon, Oxon: Routledge.

Nikkelen, S. W. C., Valkenburg, P. M., Huizinga, M., & Bushman, B. J. (2014). Media use and ADHD-related behaviors in children and adolescents: A meta-analysis. Developmental Psychology, 50 (9), 2228–2241.

Ostermayer, E. (2013). Pikler (1. Aufl). Frühe Kindheit: Pädagogische Ansätze für die Kita. Berlin: Cornelsen.

Perry, B. D. (2002). Childhood experience and the expression of genetic potential: What childhood neglect tells us about nature and nurture. Brain and Mind, 3, 79–100.

Petitmengin, C. (2007). Towards the source of thoughts: The gestural and transmodal dimension of lived experience. Journal of Consciousness Studies, 14, 54–82.

Piaget, J. (2003). Nachahmung, Spiel und Traum: Die Entwicklung der Symbolfunktion beim Kinde (5. Aufl). Gesammelte Werke: Studienausgabe / Jean Piaget; Bd. 5. Stuttgart: Klett-Cotta.

Pieters, S., Desoete, A., Roeyers, H., Vanderswalmen, R., & van Waelvelde, H. (2012). Behind mathematical learning disabilities: What about visual perception and motor skills? Learning and Individual Differences, 22 (4), 498–504.

Pin, T., Eldridge, B., & Galea, M. P. (2007). A review of the effects of sleep position, play position, and equipment use on motor development. Developmental Medicine and Child Neurology, 49, 858–867.

Plato. (2012). Republic. Harmondsworth: Penguin.

Polka, L., Rvachew, S., & Mattock, K. (2009). Experiential influences on speech perception and speech production in infancy. In E. Hoff & M. Shatz (Eds.), Blackwell handbook of language development (pp. 153–172). Chichester: Wiley-Blackwell.

Pramling, I. (2004). Demokratie: Leitprinzip des vorschulischen Bildungsplans in Schweden. In W. E. Fthenakis & P. Oberhuemer (Eds.), Frühpädagogik international: Bildungsqualität im Blickpunkt (pp. 161–173). Wiesbaden, s.l.: VS Verlag für Sozialwissenschaften.

Pulvermuller, F. (2005). Brain mechanisms linking language and action. Nature Reviews Neuroscience, July (6), 576–582.

Pulvermuller, F., Harle, M., & Hummel, F. (2001). Walking or talking? Behavioral and neurophysiological correlates of action verb processing. Brain and Language, 78 (2), 143–168.

Reganold, J. P. (1995). Soil quality and profitability of biodynamic and conventional farming systems: A review. American Journal of Alternative Agriculture, 10 (1), 36–45; available at goo.gl/RuwTG5 (accessed 8 October 2018).

Reganold, J. P., Palmer, A. S., Lockhart, J. C., & Macgregor, A. N. (1993). Soil quality and financial performance of biodynamic and conventional farms in New Zealand. Science, 260 (5106), 344–349.

Rentschler, I. (2004). Development of configural 3D object recognition. Behavioural Brain Research, 149 (1), 107–111.

Rose, M. (2007). Living literacy: The human foundations of speaking writing and reading. Stroud: Hawthorn Press.

Rose, R. (2013). Transforming criticisms of Anthroposophy and Waldorf education: Evolution, race and the quest for global ethics. Centre for Philosophy and Anthroposophy, privately published, 203pp, available online at goo.gl/STZtua.

Rose, S. E., Jolley, R. P., & Charman, A. (2012). An investigation of the expressive and representational drawing development in National Curriculum, Steiner, and Montessori schools. Psychology of Aesthetics, Creativity, and the Arts, 6 (1), 83–95.

Rosebury, S., Hirsh-Pasek, K., Parish-Morris, J., & Golinkoff, R. M. (2009). Live action: Can young children learn verbs from video? Child Development, 80 (5), 1360–1375.

Rosenberg, A. (2012). Philosophy of science: A contemporary introduction (3rd edn). London: Routledge.

Ruben, R. J. (1997). A time frame of critical/sensitive periods of language development. Acta Otolaryngologica, 117, 202–205.

Sacks, O. (2015). The man who mistook his wife for a hat. London: Picador.

Sadoski, M. & Paivio, A. (2013). Imagery and text: A dual coding theory of reading and writing (2nd edn). New York: Routledge.

Saman, Y., Bamiou, D. E., Gleeson, M., & Dutia, M. B. (2012). Interactions between stress and vestibular compensation – a review. Frontiers in Neurology, 3, 116.

Sanz-Cervera, P., Pastor-Cerezuela, G., González-Sala, F., Tárraga-Mínguez, R., & Fernández-Andrés, M.-I. (2017). Sensory processing in children with autism spectrum disorder and/or attention deficit hyperactivity disorder in the home and classroom contexts. Frontiers in Psychology, 8, 1772.

Sardello, R. & Sanders, C. (1999). Care of the senses: A neglected dimension of education. In J. Kane (Ed.), Education, information, and imagination: Essays on learning and thinking (pp. 223–247). Columbus, OH: Prentice-Hall/Merril.

Schepers, R. J. & Ringkamp, M. (2009). Thermoreceptors and thermosensitive afferents. Neuroscience and Biobehavioral Reviews, 33 (3), 205–212.

Schiller, F. (1795/2009). Über die ästhetische Erziehung des Menschen [Letters on the aesthetic education of man]. Stuttgart. Verlag Freies Geistesleben.

Schmidt, M. E., Pempek, T. A., Kirkorian, H. L., Lund, A. F., & Anderson, D. R. (2008). The effects of background television on the toy play behavior of very young children. Child Development, 79 (4), 1137–1151.

Schreier, U. & Association Soin de la Terre. (2015). Biodynamics a promising road to tomorrow's sustainable agriculture. Association Soin de la Terre; available from goo.gl/5xock9 (accessed 5 October 2018).

Schweinhart, L. J., & Weikart, D. P. (1997). The High/Scope preschool curriculum comparison study through age 23. Early Childhood Research Quarterly, 12, 117–143.

Seamon, D. & Zajonc, A. (Eds.). (1998). Goethe's way of science: A phenomenology of nature. Albany: State University of New York Press.

Sekuler, R. & Blake, R. (2002). Perception (4th edn). Boston: McGraw-Hill.

Selg, P. (2017). The child as a sense organ: An anthroposophic understanding of imitation processes. Great Barrington, Mass.: SteinerBooks.

Shapiro, L. (2011). Embodied cognition. Abingdon, Oxon: Routledge.

Sheets-Johnstone, M. (2010). Body and movement: Basic dynamic principles. In S. Gallagher (Ed.), Handbook of phenomenology and cognitive science (pp. 217–234). Dordrecht: Springer.

Shum, S. B. M. & Pang, M. Y. C. (2009). Children with attention deficit hyperactivity disorder have impaired balance function: Involvement of somatosensory, visual, and vestibular systems. Journal of Pediatrics, 155 (2), 245–249.

Skeldon, A. C., Phillips, A. J. K., & Dijk, D.-J. (2017). The effects of self-selected light-dark cycles and social constraints on human sleep and circadian timing: A modeling approach. Scientific Reports, 7, 45158.

Slater, A., Brown, E., & Badenoch, M. (1997). Intermodal perception at birth: Newborn infants' memory for arbitrary auditory–visual pairings. Early Development and Parenting, 6 (3–4), 99–104.

Smits, S. A., Leach, J., Sonnenburg, E. D., & others (2017). Seasonal cycling in the gut microbiome of the Hadza hunter-gatherers of Tanzania. Science, 357, 802–806.

Soesman, A. (2000). Our twelve senses: How healthy senses refresh the soul: An introduction to anthroposophy and spiritual psychology based on Rudolf Steiner's studies of the senses. Stroud: Hawthorn Press.

Soil Association. (2001). Organic farming, food quality and human health. A review of the evidence. Bristol: Soil Association; available from goo. gl/rKGAEu (accessed 5 October 2018).

Steiner, R. (1914/1994). Theosophy: An introduction to the spiritual processes in human life and in the cosmos. Hudson, NY: Anthroposophic Press.

Steiner, R. (1917/1996). Riddles of the soul. Spring Valley: Mercury Press.

Steiner, R. (1918/1986). Die Philosophie der Freiheit [The Philosophy of Freedom]. Dornach, Switzerland: Rudolf Steiner Verlag.

Steiner, R. (1919/1993). Allgemeine Menschenkunde als Grundlage der Pädagogik (Study of Man) ([51.–60. Tsd.]). Rudolf Steiner Taschenbücher aus dem Gesamtwerk: Vol. 617. Dornach: R. Steiner Verlag.

Steiner, R. (1919/2000). Practical advice to teachers. Great Barrington, Mass.: Anthroposophic Press.

Steiner, R. (1921–1922/2003). Soul economy: Body, soul, and spirit in Waldorf education. Great Barrington, Mass.: Anthroposophic Press

Steiner, R. (1924). Mein Lebensgang [The course of my life]. Dornach.

Steiner, R. (1925/1989). Anthroposophische Leitsätze [Anthroposophical leading thoughts] (9th edn). Dornach: Rudolf Steiner Verlag.

Steiner, R. (1923/1996). The child's changing consciousness: As the basis of pedagogical practice. Hudson, NY: Anthroposophic Press.

Steiner, R. (1909/1996a). The spiritual hierarchies and the physical world: Reality and illusion. Hudson, NY: Anthroposophic Press.

Steiner, R. (1919/1996b). The foundations of human experience. Hudson, NY: Anthroposophic Press.

Steiner, R. (1925/1997). An outline of esoteric science. Classics in anthroposophy. Hudson, NY: Anthroposophic Press.

Steiner, R. (1998). Guidance in esoteric training: From the Esoteric School (3rd edn). London: Rudolf Steiner Press.

Steiner, R. (1999). A psychology of body, soul, and spirit: Anthroposophy, psychosophy, and pneumatosophy: twelve lectures, Berlin, October 23–27, 1909, November 1–4, 1910, December 12–16, 1911. Hudson, NY: Anthroposophic Press.

Steiner, R. (1924/2004). Human values in education: 10 lectures in Arnheim, Holland; July 17–24, 1924 (rev. edn). Great Barrington, Mass.: Anthroposophic Press.

Steiner, R. (1919/2008). How to know higher worlds. Radford, VA: Wilder Publications.

Steiner, R. (Ed.). (2009). Anthroposophie: Ein Fragment (5. Aufl.). Gesamtausgabe Schriften Veröffentlichungen aus dem Nachlass: III. Dornach: Rudolf-Steiner-Verl.

Stenius, F., Swartz, J., Lindblad, F., & others (2010). Low salivary cortisol levels in infants of families with an anthroposophic lifestyle. Psychoneuroendocrinology, 35 (10), 1431–1437.

Suggate, S. P. (2009). School entry age and reading achievement in the 2006 Programme for International Student Assessment (PISA). International Journal of Educational Research, 48, 151–161.

Suggate, S. P. (2010). Why 'what' we teach depends on 'when': Grade and reading intervention modality moderate effect size. Developmental Psychology, 46, 1556–1579.

Suggate, S. P. (2011). Viewing the long-term effects of early reading with an open eye. In R. House (Ed.), Too much, too soon? Early learning and the erosion of childhood (pp. 236–246). Stroud: Hawthorn Press.

Suggate, S. P. (2012). Watering the garden before a rainstorm: The case of early reading. In S. P. Suggate & E. Reese (Eds.), Contemporary debates in child development and education (pp. 181–190). London: Routledge.

Suggate, S. P. (2015). The Parable of the Sower and the long-term effects of early reading. European Early Childhood Education Research Journal, 23, 524–544.

Suggate, S. P. (2016). A meta-analysis of the long-term effects of phonemic awareness, phonics, fluency, and reading comprehension interventions. Journal of Learning Disabilities, 49, 77–96.

Suggate, S. & Stoeger, H. (2017). Fine motor skills enhance lexical processing of embodied vocabulary: A test of the nimble-hands, nimble-minds hypothesis. Quarterly Journal of Experimental Psychology, 70, 2169–2187.

Suggate, S. P., Pufke, E., & Stoeger, H. (2016). The effect of fine and grapho-motor skill demands on preschoolers' decoding skill. Journal of Experimental Child Psychology, 141, 34–48.

Suggate, S. P., Schaughency, E. A., & Reese, E. (2013). Children who learn to read later catch up to children who learn to read early. Early Childhood Research Quarterly, 23, 33–48.

Suggate, S. P., Stoeger, H., & Fischer, U. (2017). Fine motor skills predict finger-based numerical skills in preschoolers. Perceptual and Motor Skills, 124, 1085-1106.

Suggate, S. P., Lenhard, W., Neudecker, E., & Schneider, W. (2013). Incidental vocabulary acquisition from stories: Second and fourth graders learn more from listening than reading. First Language, 33, 551–571.

Suggate, S., Schaughency, E., McAnally, H., & Reese, E. (2018). From infancy to adolescence: The longitudinal links between vocabulary, early literacy skills, oral narrative, and reading comprehension. Cognitive Development, 47, 82–95.

Tager-Flusberg, H. (2009). Atypical language development: Autism and other neurodevelopmental disorders. In E. Hoff & M. Shatz (Eds.), Blackwell handbook of language development (pp. 432–453). Chichester: Wiley-Blackwell.

Taylor, A. F., Kuo, F. E., & Sullivan, W. C. (2001). Coping with ADD: The surprising connection to green play settings. Environment and Behavior, 33, 54–77.

Taylor, M. (Ed.). (2013). Oxford handbook of the development of imagination. Oxford: Oxford University Press.

Thelen, E. (2000). Grounded in the world: Developmental origins of the embodied mind. Infancy, 1, 3–28.

Trachtenberg, J. T. (2015). Competition, inhibition, and critical periods of cortical plasticity. Current Opinion in Neurobiology, 35, 44–48.

Trettenbrein, P. C. (2016). The demise of the synapse as the locus of memory: A looming paradigm shift? Frontiers in Systems Neuroscience, 10, 88.

Trionfi, G. & Reese, E. (2009). A good story: Children with imaginary companions create richer narratives. Child Development, 80, 1301–1313.

Trousselard, M., Barraud, P., Nougier, V., Raphel, C., & Cian, C. (2004). Contribution of tactile and interoceptive cues to the perception of the direction of gravity. Cognitive Brain Research, 20 (3), 355–362.

Vaahtoranta, E., Suggate, S., Jachmann, C., Lenhart, J., & Lenhard, W. (2017). Can explaining less be more? Enhancing vocabulary through explicit versus elaborative storytelling. First Language, 38 (2), 198–217.

Valkenburg, P. M. & van der Voort, T. H. A. (1994). Influence of TV on daydreaming and creative imagination: A review of research. Psychological Bulletin, 116 (2), 316–339.

Valkenburg, P. M. & van der Voort, T. H. A. (1995). The influence of television on children's daydreaming styles: A 1-year panel study. Communication Research, 22 (3), 267–287.

Vandewalle, G., Gais, S., Schabus, M., & others (2007). Wavelength-dependent modulation of brain responses to a working memory task by daytime light exposure. Cerebral Cortex, 17 (12), 2788–2795.

Vinter, A. & Chartrel, E. (2008). Visual and proprioceptive recognition of cursive letters in young children. Acta Psychologica, 129 (1), 147–156.

von Kügelgen, H. (1993). The history of the Waldorf kindergartens and the International Waldorf Kindergarten Association. In J. Almon (Ed.), An overview of the Waldorf Kindergarten (vol. 1). Silver Spring, MD: Waldorf Kindergarten Association.

Vriens, J., Nilius, B., & Voets, T. (2014). Peripheral thermosensation in mammals. Nature Reviews, Neuroscience, 15 (9), 573–589.

Wade, N. (2005). Your body is younger than you think. New York Times, 2 August.

Waite, S. & Rees, S. (2011). Imagination in Steiner kindergartens: Practices and potential purposes. In R. Parker-Rees (Ed.), Meeting the child in Steiner kindergartens: An exploration of beliefs, values, and practices (pp. 51–67). London: Routledge.

Wallace, C. E. & Russ, S. W. (2015). Pretend play, divergent thinking, and math achievement in girls: A longitudinal study. Psychology of Aesthetics, Creativity, and the Arts, 9 (3), 296–305.

Walter, H. (2012). Social cognitive neuroscience of empathy: Concepts, circuits, and genes. Emotion Review, 4 (1), 9–17.

Wamain, Y., Tallet, J., Zanone, P.-G., & Longcamp, M. (2012). Brain responses to handwritten and printed letters differentially depend on the activation state of the primary motor cortex. NeuroImage, 63 (3), 1766–1773.

Weis, R. & Cerankosky, B. C. (2010). Effects of video-game ownership on young boys' academic and behavioral functioning: A randomized, controlled study. Psychological Science, 21 (4), 463–470.

Weisberg, D. S., Hirsh-Pasek, K., Golinkoff, R. M., Kittredge, A. K., & Klahr, D. (2016). Guided play. Current Directions in Psychological Science, 25 (3), 177–182.

Weisberg, D. S., Ilgaz, H., Hirsh-Pasek, K., & others (2015). Shovels and swords: How realistic and fantastical themes affect children's word learning. Cognitive Development, 35, 1–14.

Westendorp, M., Hartman, E., Houwen, S., Smith, J., & Visscher, C. (2011). The relationship between gross motor skills and academic achievement in children with learning disabilities. Research in Developmental Disabilities, 32 (6), 2773–2779.

Wolff, O. (1988). Soziale Hygiene: Ursachen, Wesen und Bewältigung e. Zivilisationskrankheit. Bad Liebenzell-Unterlengenhardt: Verein für Anthroposophisches Heilwesen.

Wolff, O. (2007). Die naturgemässe Hausapotheke: Praktischer Ratgeber für Gesundheit und Krankheit. Praxis Anthroposophie: Vol. 79. Stuttgart: Verl. Freies Geistesleben.

Wolff, O. (2012). Was essen wir eigentlich? Praktische Gesichtspunkte zur Ernährung (3rd revised edn.). Stuttgart: Verl. Freies Geistesleben.

Yang, F., Helgason, A. R., Sigfusdottir, I. D., & Kristjansson, A. L. (2013). Electronic screen use and mental well-being of 10–12 year-old children. European Journal of Public Health, 23 (3), 492–498.

Youngstedt, S. D., Goff, E. E., Reynolds, A. M., & others (2016). Has adult sleep duration declined over the last 50+ years? Sleep Medicine Reviews, 28, 69–85.

Yuan, K., Qin, W., Wang, G., & others (2011). Microstructure abnormalities in adolescents with internet addiction disorder. PloS One, 6 (6), e20708.

Zack, E., Barr, R., Gerhardstein, P., Dickerson, K., & Meltzoff, A. N. (2009). Infant imitation from television using novel touch screen technology. British Journal of Developmental Psychology, 27 (1), 13–26.

Zimmerman, F. J. & Christakis, D. A. (2005). Children's television viewing and cognitive outcomes: A longitudinal analysis of national data. Archives of Pediatric Adolescent Medicine, 159 (619–625).

Zimmerman, F. J., Christakis, D. A., & Meltzoff, A. N. (2007). Associations between media viewing and language development in children under age 2 years. Journal of Pediatrics, 151 (4), 364–368.

Zoia, S., Blason, L., D'Ottavio, G., & others(2007). Evidence of early development of action planning in the human foetus: A kinematic study. Experimental Brain Research, 176 (2), 217–226.

Zwaan, R. A. & Taylor, L. J. (2006). Seeing, acting, understanding: Motor resonance in language comprehension. Journal of Experimental Psychology: General, 135 (1), 1–11.

Index

A

academic push, 138

activity
see movement, purposeful activity

ADHD
see Attention Deficit Hyperactivity Disorder

adolescence, 66

Advent Spiral, 119

aesthetic experiences, 82–7

African fairy tales, 131

allergies to milk and wheat, 101

Alliance for Childhood, xvi

Almon, J., xv–xvi

amylase (enzyme), 97

anomia, 48–9

anthroposophy, 2;
arising from philosophy, 6–9;
defined, 8;
demystified, 5–15;
education arising from, 9–11;
spirituality/religion and, 142–4;
threefold human being in, 24–6;
view of the human being, 17–30;
view of human development, 59–66;
see also
General Anthroposophical Society

antipathy, 27, 153n;
and 'I' sense, 53

anxiety, xvi;
and balance, 40

architecture
of the kindergarten, 113–14

Argaman kindergarten (Israel), 122–4

Aristotle, 23, 42

arts (the), 82–7 *passim*;
artistic activities, 82–4;
'domestic', 106

assessment culture, 136

Association of Waldorf Kindergartens, 112

atmosphere, 91

Attention Deficit Hyperactivity Disorder (ADHD), 40

auditory sense, 46–7

authority, 153n

autism, 52, 54, 72

avoiding explanations, 63

B

balance
anxiety and, 40;
sense of, 39–40

Bastian, H., 38

Baxter, C., 37

behaviourism, 58

binding problem (the), 153n

biodynamic food, 97, 98

birthdays, 119

body (the), 24, 25;
'schema', 30;
see also movement

brain (the), 7, 17, 20, 67;
early growth, 64;
see also neuropsychological revolution

breathing in/breathing out, 88

Brentano, C., 46

distraction, 104;
    redirecting a game, 104

distraction, 104

disturbed senses, 72

Divali festival, 119, 122

dolls: *see* Waldorf dolls

'domestic arts' (Nicol), 106

'drop of golden oil' ritual, 94

Drummond, M.J., 76, 91, 105, 106

dualism, 17

E

early academic focus, 144–6

early childhood development, 62–5

early 'gains', xvi

Early Years Foundation Stage
    profile, 105

Easter, 129

eating
    purpose of, 95;
    and rhythm, 98–9;
    see also digestion, food, gluten
    intolerance, nutrition, obesity

education
    anthroposphy arising from, 9–11;
    narrow conceptions of, 5;
    see also educational principles,
    Steiner education

educational goals: meeting, 124

educational principles
    (Waldorf-Steiner), 75–110;
    aesthetic experiences, 82–7;
    imagination/free play, 79–82;
    imitation, 76–9;
    relating to the child, 102–6;

rhythm/security, 87–94;
    self-development/reflection, 106–10;
    whole nutrition, 94–101

electronic media/devices, 89, 135, 146–9;
    and addiction, 148;
    and imagination, 80;
    negative effects of, 148;
    and sensory development, 149;
    see also screen time, technology

Eliot, T.S., 47

embodied cognition, 51

empathy
    consistency with 'I' sense, 54;
    research on, 54

environment
    ordered, 91–2;
    as third teacher, 113–15

Errenst, M, 152n

eurythmy, 154n

executive functioning, 61

EYFS:
    see Early Years Foundation Stage

F

family involvement, 119;
    see also parents

feeling, 26–30 *passim*;
    relationship to past/future, 27;
    senses, 40–5

festival celebrations, 83, 122–3,
    128–30, 143;
    Christian, 119;
    Divali, 119;
    Hannukah, 119;
    St John's Day, 119, 129–30;
    Tihar, 125–6;
    see also ceremony, Christmas, Easter

Finland, 136

food
biodynamic, 97, 98;
highly processed, 99;
organic, 97–8;
overabundance of, 98
preparation, 95–6;
'synergy', 97;
see also digestion, eating, gluten
intolerance, meal-time, nutrition,
sourdough, sugar, wheat

forest kindergartens, 133–4

formal education, 137

Foundations of human experience, The
(Steiner), 112

Frankl, V., 89

free play: see play

freedom, 153n;
distinguished from freehood, 60–1;
educating for, 75–110 *passim*;
excessive (Plato), 136;
Steiner's views on, 60;
see also freehood, Philosophy of
Freedom

freehood, 73;
developing, 60–2;
distinguished from freedom, 60–1

Freud, S., 23

Fröbel, F., 111

G

Gallagher, S., 30

Gallese, V., 53–4

gardening, 89–90
see also nature

General Anthroposophical Society, 144

gestures, 87

gluten intolerance, 101

goals: *see* educational goals

Goethe, J.W. von, 18, 34, 42, 67;
colour theory of, 115;
on light, 34

Goetheanum (the), 14, 114

Goodhall, R., 130

gout, 98

Grunelius, von, E., 113, 114

gustation, 41–2

H

Hahn, H., 81

Hannukah festival, 119, 123

health: *see* children's health, healthy
diet, well-being

healthy diet, 96

Heine, H., 44

historical development of Waldorf-
Steiner, 111–12

home visits, 109

How to know higher worlds
(Steiner), 107

Howard, Sir A., 96

human being
anthroposophical view of the, 17–30;
threefold conception of, 18, 22–4

human development
anthroposophical lifespan
view of, 59–6;
see also child development,
development, self-development

warmth
  sense of, 44–5

well-being
  sense of, 37;
  see also health

wheat, 100–1:
  allergies to, 101;
  digestion of, 100;
  preparation of, 101

Wilderspin, S., 111

will (the), 63, 135–6:
  educating, 28–30 *passim*;
  strengthening the, 152n;
  unconscious nature of, 27, 29, 63

William's syndrome, 52, 54

willing, 26–30 *passim*;
  senses, 35–40;
  see also will (the)

Wilson, M., 153n

Wilson, W., 154n

Winter Garden (prologue), xvii

Wolakota Waldorf kindergarten, 121

Wolff, O., 94, 98, 99, 100, 101

wonder
  natural state of, 113

Y

Yemini, N., 122–4

About the Authors

Sebastian Suggate, Ph.D., born 1981, is a lecturer in education at the University of Regensburg, Germany. He was born in New Zealand where he studied psychology, receiving his Ph.D. in 2009 from the University of Otago. In 2010 he moved to Germany, working as an Alexander-von-Humboldt post-doctoral researcher at the University of Würzburg. Subsequent to a first stint in Regensburg, he was a professor in developmental psychology and education at Alanus University, where he was also involved in training Waldorf kindergarten teachers. His research focuses on children's language, fine motor skills, electronic media and reading development.

Tamara Suggate, M.Sc, born 1984, is currently employed in a Steiner kindergarten in Regensburg, Germany. She was born in England before emigrating to New Zealand as a child. She also studied at the University of Otago, receiving a Masters in Psychology in 2009. In 2010 she moved with her husband and then two daughters to Germany, where two further daughters were born. All their children have attended, or do attend, Steiner schools/kindergartens. Both Tamara and Sebastian have been involved in founding a new Waldorf school and kindergarten in Regensburg.

ORDERING BOOKS

•

If you have difficulties ordering Hawthorn Press books
from a bookshop, you can order direct from our website
www.hawthornpress.com, or from our UK distributor
BookSource: 50 Cambuslang Road, Glasgow, G32 8NB:
Tel: (0845) 370 0063, E-mail: orders@booksource.net.

Details of our overseas distributors can be found on our website.

Hawthorn Press
www.hawthornpress.com